For Brett
With all best wishes
Mark

# CHRISTIANIA

## 50TH ANNIVERSARY EDITION

**MARK EDWARDS**

*Christiania* was first published in Danish by Informations Forlag in 1979. It was translated into German by Rowohlt Verlag GmbH and published in 1980.

Published in English in 2021 by Hard Rain Trading Company.

*Christiania: 50th Anniversary Edition* is produced by Mark Edwards and Mike Kenny in a limited edition of 2000 copies. We bypassed commercial publishers to keep control over the printing and make the book available at the lowest possible price. It is available from shops in Christiania and online at www.christiania.co.uk where the pictures and text can be viewed free of charge for those who do not want to buy the book.

Photographs and text © copyright Mark Edwards
Editor: Kristina Blagojevitch
Design: Mike Kenny
Printed in Slovenia by LUart d.o.o.

ISBN 978-1-905588-05-3

Do send your comments about this edition as well as your recollections, stories and thoughts about Christiania to mark@hardrainproject.com.

If the book, posters and postcards make a profit it will be donated to the Hard Rain Project charity. We work with artists and scientists to promote solutions that address the broad challenges of climate change, poverty eradication, environmental protection and sustainable consumption: www.hardrainproject.com

# CONTENTS

# PREFACE TO CHRISTIANIA: 50TH ANNIVERSARY EDITION

Christiania, an island completely surrounded by Denmark, celebrates its 50th anniversary in September 2021.

Nicholas Albery, chronicler of Britain's 'alternative movement', back in the day, called Christiania 'the seventh wonder of the alternative world— one of the most important experiments in human relationships taking place'. Others argue that Christiania is irrelevant because its relationship with the state will never be extended to other communities. It cannot be cloned. But that's what makes Christiania unique; nothing like it exists anywhere else in the world.

Christiania, also known as the Freetown, occupies an abandoned military complex in the Christianshavn neighbourhood of Copenhagen, just a few minutes' cycle ride from the Danish parliament. Its 7.7 hectares (19 acres) include parkland, a lake and many historic buildings and ramparts dating back to the 17th century. Its very international community consists of about 1,500 residents.

The story begins on 4th September 1971. People living around the abandoned barracks broke through the fence to take over the area as a playground for their children. More ambitious plans for the site were announced a few weeks later by Jacob Ludvigsen, a well-known figure in the Danish alternative lifestyle movement and founder of the weekly magazine, *Hovedbladet*, when he and five friends took a picnic to the barracks to proclaim the Free City of Christiania an 'experiment in living' on 26th September. Jacob's now famous article appeared in the 2nd October issue of *Hovedbladet*:

> Christiania is a land for settlers. It is the biggest opportunity so far to build a society from scratch while using existing buildings. For those who feel the beating of the pioneer heart there can be no doubt as to the purpose of Christiania.

The call was irresistible. Artists, hippies, builders, bakers, candlestick makers, crazy people, hash dealers, romantics, activists, inactivists, refugees, idealists and those whose wounds could not be healed moved in. These pioneers set about solving the practical problems of converting military buildings into homes and the even more daunting challenge of establishing a self-governing alternative community.

They also had to negotiate a treaty with the government that would allow the settlers to stay. Perhaps they took heed of the May '68 slogan: 'Be reasonable—demand the impossible.' If so, they succeeded where the French students had failed. It was agreed that the Freetown could be regarded as a social experiment; much of the administration usually involved in the running of a modern, highly regulated society would not be enforced in Christiania—most of the time.

But at the heart of the Freetown was a paradox: Christianites wanted more out of life than rush hours and the daily grind but were dependent on the support that a modern, wealthy economy created. The agreement Christiania broadly accepted was an attempt to balance the equation. Ole Espersen, Minister of Justice, 1981–1982, saw Christiania as a place where new ways of living could be tried.

> In all big cities there are areas with serious problems. In Denmark, we've usually tried to solve them through legislation, backed up by official institutions. People in Christiania respond to problems directly—person to person—by taking care of each other. This is a reaction against professional social workers, and my hope is that the positive aspects of Christiania will spread to other places and complement professional social workers and institutions.

Christiania didn't develop a constitution (perish the thought), but area meetings were held and occasionally meetings for the whole community were called. People had the opportunity to speak up for the kind of community they wanted. Not everyone participated, but many people found their voice for the first time in Christiania's meetings.

I took the photographs in this book between 1976 and 1979, and was the first photographer to be given 'all area access' to the Freetown. This unofficial permission wasn't granted easily—nor should it have been. There's a fine line between photographing a community in an exploitative way and making an intimate record of people who wanted to challenge themselves and the society they had rejected. I had to show that I understood the boundaries. Each time I returned, I gave pictures from the previous trip to their subjects. Gradually doors opened, allowing me to make a unique record of a remarkable community in its formative years.

This anniversary edition is based on the original Danish book published in 1979. I've not updated my account to include changes that have taken place since I left, but while in coronavirus lockdown, I went back to the original contact prints and re-edited the photographs I had taken. If you compare this edition with the original, you'll notice several 'new' pictures—that is, photos that I took back then but am publishing for the first time now. How did I miss them first time around? Honestly, I don't know… but here they are, as fresh as the day they appeared in my viewfinder.

I have also rearranged the photo sequence. If, as I hope, you look at photo books from start to finish, the pictures will take you around the public places in the Freetown, and when you have your bearings, you can visit some of its early residents in their homes and workshops and get a glimpse of the night life.

I also recorded conversations with some of Christiania's pioneers for the Danish edition of the book and include them here (lightly edited) in sections rather than interspersed with the pictures. I can't read Danish, so I've not read the text since I handed over the English manuscript to Informations Forlag's editor, Per Kofod, for translation. I was fascinated to read them again. The Christiania tapes are moving, funny, heartbreaking, sometimes all at the same time. Above all they are honest, painfully so at times. They demonstrate a rare confidence that Christiania fostered within its community. People weren't judged by the standards set by society at large. There was always a redeeming aspect to be found, and this tended to bolster confidence and bring out the best in everyone.

I'm writing about Christiania in the past tense. My life took a different direction after the book came out, and I gradually lost touch with the community, but the Freetown has famously survived against the odds. This is a tribute to its inhabitants, of course, but also to the spirit of tolerance that permeates Danish society.

Let's also acknowledge the difficulty any government would face in evicting a thousand people, their children, dogs, cats, horses, livestock, several monkeys—even a grumpy bear—from an unofficial World Heritage site that can summon celebrity and public support from Europe and beyond. Even Christiania's most vocal critics in government couldn't imagine carrying out a forced eviction. This was Christiania's trump card; it provided the community with an uneasy security.

I wrote in the original edition: *This book is as different from Christiania as a map is from the city. It contains some 400 photographs, the combined exposure time was about three seconds. You are witnessing three seconds, carefully selected from the eighteen months I spent in Christiania!*

If you lived in the Freetown in the 1970s, those three seconds and the stories you or your friends told me of your lives might tug at your memories. It was a special time for all of us.

If you're a visitor to Christiania, looking at these pages half a century later, they might help you understand why refugees from Europe and beyond were attracted to the community. The Freetown offered a safe testing ground where the dreams and aspirations of the 1960s counterculture could collide with the reality of human nature.

But dreams and reality make strange bedfellows, and so it was in Christiania. Many people moving to the Freetown had been badly let down by official institutions, or their parents and teachers. They found a home in Christiania, and many benefited from the freewheeling approach. But not everyone. A TV documentary gave a platform to some of the children who grew up in the Freetown who were failed by their parents and the wider Christiania community.[1] Here we are reminded

that people on either side of the boundary that separates the Freetown from 'the outside' are more alike than unalike. No one neighbourhood has all the answers—there are heartbreaking failures on both sides of the fence which warn against inflated claims for one system or another.

But revisiting this period, as I am doing, in the midst of a pandemic, I am struck by the extraordinary contrast between now and then. The pictures and interviews mostly reflect the optimism and imagination that energised the youth movement all those years ago. We didn't believe governments could deliver the world we wanted, so we set about creating it in our own back yards. The counterculture absorbed and renewed the values of romanticism, bohemianism and pacifism. Organised religions and nationalism were disparaged. A strong interest in Eastern mysticism[2] developed, along with a growing concern for the natural environment. This led to the founding of campaign groups, including Greenpeace and Friends of the Earth, which demanded a new sense of shared interest, a new and vital human togetherness to protect nature and civilisation.[3]

Part of that cultural wave was about the freedom to realise our desires, but the youth movement broke down some of the class barriers and racial divisions that afflicted society.[4] It was sustained by the arts, especially popular music, and amplified (and frequently distorted) by the media, eager to present this new cultural landscape to a wider public. I also felt that photographing Christiania was an opportunity to reflect the wider counterculture values I grew up with.

This was the time when mainstream Western society had embarked on a wave of consumerism the like of which had never before been witnessed. In the 50 years since Christiania was founded, humans have used more resources than in all previous history.[5] The effect of this 'development' is now apparent—even to its most committed advocates:

1   *Children of the Hippies*. Director: Nille Westh. Produced by DR, 2015.

2   Peter Washington in his wonderful book, *Madam Blavatsky's Baboon*, traces the roots of the New Age to the Theosophical Society co-founded by Madam Blavatsky.

3   It should be noted that Christiania fostered a brand of nationalism with its own flag and patriotic songs. The structures of identity had simply been transferred from the state to the Freetown.

4   The terrible irony of the Black Lives Matter slogan—the need to insist on what ought to be obvious, shows that a more profound transformation is called for if humanity is to extend the most basic rights of equality to all its citizens.

5   *Whole Earth? Aligning Human Systems and Natural Systems* by Mark Edwards & Lloyd Timberlake. Published by Hard Rain Project ISBN 9781905588046.

climate change, destruction of ecosystems, pollution and overpopulation are problems threatening our civilisation, and perhaps the human race and our planet itself, with almost total annihilation.

What's called for now is a surge of creativity not just in science and the arts but in every sphere of human life. Something along those lines—a radical transformation that included science, art and a new view of humanity, culture and society—must have taken place in the Renaissance. We saw an echo of this in the 1960s, along with a growing awareness of the need for a radically new, worldwide approach.

Once again, the world looks to young people who have the courage to be different. There are lessons here for a new generation of school students who understand the acute danger we are all in, as governments, corporations and the silent majority lead humanity to the edge of environmental catastrophe.

At the heart of Christiania's offer is a greater emphasis on community life, education and the arts rather than the pursuit of material wealth. But Christiania also shows the pitfalls a freewheeling community has to deal with if it is to contribute to the immense challenges the next 50 years will bring.

Mark Edwards, London, 9th March 2021

I described Christiania in a letter to fellow photographer, Chris Steele-Perkins, in 1978. It reveals something of the way I lived in the Freetown and some of my attitudes and prejudices.

Dear Chris,
I thought you might be interested to hear about Christiania and now's a good time to write, because I've been living here for the last couple of months without being a photographer, so I have a different view of the community. It's been good to just talk to people without that glance at the background or the search for a revealing expression which makes for good photographs but keeps you at a distance.

My truck is parked behind a lovely old building called Kosmiske Blomst. An estate agent's description might read something like this: 'Historic, late eighteenth-century farmhouse with commanding view of seventeenth-century moat. Thirty metres of private frontage to mooring. Delightful, informal gardens. Conveniently situated fifteen minutes from the centre of Copenhagen. Retains all original features, leaving scope for modernisation.' The building was originally part of the outer defences of Copenhagen and at first it was just a wall with slits for soldiers to point guns towards Sweden. Then, in 1779, another building was constructed around the wall, and it was used for storing gunpowder and ammunition until the army left the area a few years ago. It's right on the edge of the lake, surrounded by trees, with just the distant sound of traffic to remind you that you are close to the centre of Copenhagen.

Seven people live here, each in their own room, and right now there are good feelings between everyone. A lot of music and good conversation. It's very luxurious, even without water and electricity.

In winter, big wood-burning stoves provide heat. The wood is free, delivered to Christiania by demolition contractors who are pulling down the old buildings in the city.

Last summer I used to get up early, take a camera and six rolls of film, and walk around Christiania all day. I spent every moment looking for pictures. At night I just switched cameras and carried on with infrared film and Weegee-inspired 'invisible' flash. I kept going eighteen hours a day! I probably cut a slightly comical figure but against the background of Christiania I didn't feel out of place. By this time, I was just allowed to do whatever I wanted. Now when I wake up, I get to work with the contact sheets or the Christiania tapes. I'm also trying to write an introduction to this book in a small attic above a friend's house in Mælkebøtten.

The only photographs I'm taking at the moment are portraits. I've converted my truck into a high-class photo booth and have asked about twenty people to sit for me. They can, I think, demonstrate, in case

anyone is still not convinced, the complex mixture of personalities in Christiania. I cycle them there on my Long John, a delivery bike with a large platform between the handlebars and the front wheel, while a large dog, who's decided never to let me out of his sight, runs alongside and licks their faces. This cycle ride is something of an exercise in trust and a good beginning to the photo session.

There are things I don't like here—for instance the false belief that the whole world could be like Christiania. Here we enjoy a relatively high standard of living compared to the amount of effort we exert because we're living off the handouts from a rich society. That rich society outside enjoys a high standard of living because it's living off the Third World. Without a rich Denmark and exploited poor countries, Christiania's economy would collapse.

I also feel the government could have made a better arrangement with Christiania. If, in addition to the understanding that the laws of the land would be interpreted in a more relaxed way, they'd left the Freetown without electricity and disqualified anyone living here from state benefits and not demanded any taxes from individuals or the community, Christiania would've been forced to develop totally outside 'the system'.

Both you and I have rooms in London where we're more or less strangers to our neighbours, so you can imagine how nice it is to go out and see friendly faces. But this place is also like a refugee camp. There are people who've escaped from the capitalist world and the communist world, from mental hospitals and from broken homes, from city life and prisons and the routine of factory work—and all these experiences are thrown together in this old army camp. People have a curious composite idea of alternative communities. The question 'How do people live in Christiania?' is impossible to answer. 'What work do they do?' 'What are the houses like?' 'Do people live in couples or in groups?' Each person you ask will have their own answer. I read an interview with Alan Bean, pilot of the Apollo 12 mission to the moon, in which he said, 'Going to the moon didn't change anyone, it helped make us more ourselves.' I would say living in Christiania has rather the same effect. You're not made to conform to middle-class standards. This isn't a very profound change in itself, but it's a small step towards more honest relationships with the people around you.

People generally say that Christiania is divided into three groups: the pushers and criminals, the idealists and activists, and the 'crazies'. For the pushers and criminals, Christiania is a bit like the Wild West frontier. There's a bar called Woodstock, not a very big place, where there are about six tables. The dealers sit around with their scales and their various kinds of hash, looking tough with their leather coats and long knives. I've noticed that there's a special relationship between the dealers and the 'crazies' who hang out there; if the crazies ever need to borrow money, they're always given what they need, and no interest is charged.

There's a lot of distrust between the pushers and the activists. When you hear them talking, they sound like politicians from the left and right arguing. The activists have a vision of the future, and they want to gradually change the world so that it conforms to this vision. The pushers like the free-market system, so even alternative Christiania is divided by conventional politics.

The 'crazies' are like an extended family. Like everyone else here, they have to make a space for themselves to live in. Of course, this space is not limitless—it still has boundaries and the interesting thing is how precisely they know their boundaries. They have loosened up people in Christiania with their extreme behaviour and contributed a lot but sometimes it can be too much. Psychiatric hospitals even tell patients to go to Christiania when they discharge them. A doctor said to one person, 'If you go to Copenhagen you will last two weeks: if you go to Christiania you will last a month. You'd better go to Christiania.'

People are very generous with their time—perhaps a little less so now that there are so many people living here, but a person who really needs help will always find someone to talk to.

There are no authorities governing Christiania. There are local area meetings and common meetings, but they don't happen very often, and since anyone can speak for as long as they like, nothing much gets decided.

To describe Christiania residents as falling into one of just three groups does not give a real impression of the place—there are so many extraordinary people, living in so many different ways. I've just come from the bakery where I had breakfast with the people who worked there last night. On the way back to my room, a crazy guy wearing a crash helmet demanded I give him back his elephants (see page 129). Then he told me what he'd really lost, and said, 'I know I'm a bit too much sometimes and people try to help me, but I'm alive in this world, and I see the sun move over the moon, and I see the earth turning, and the grass growing, and I know I'm too much sometimes, but I'm alive in this world.'

The social welfare office is conveniently situated a few minutes' walk from Christiania's main gate. The economy of the Freetown is such that you can live comfortably on 350 Kr. (£35) a week—that's the amount of unemployment benefit you get. This is how it's been explained to me: 'There's not enough work in Denmark so the people who don't want to work may as well be unemployed and live in Christiania, where they can learn something about not working, or work in their own way doing something they're interested in, making things in a way that may not be economically viable by commercial standards but will be humanly satisfying.' At this point mention is usually made of a government 'cost benefit analysis' report on Christiania, showing that the Freetown saves the Danish taxpayer money overall because of the number of people who would have to be institutionalised if it was closed. See how Christiania locks into the system…

There's a lot of smoking and drinking and hanging out. A lot of people who've been pushed around all their lives find it hard going when the pressure is off. There's a bar called the Månefiskaren (Fishing for the Moon), and very late, when the townspeople have gone home and only Christianites are left, an extraordinary atmosphere develops. I don't think there can be a bar anywhere as strange as this. Crazy people turn into David Bowie, Captain Mark Phillips, or the King of Denmark. There are hippies, criminals, intellectuals, Danish rockers, runaway kids, dogs, punks, drunks, homosexuals… A few minutes away is Christiania's Dante's Inferno, Fælleskøkkenet (the community kitchen). It sells cooked food (not great) and sandwiches (excellent), and as in Woodstock, hash imported from all over the world. You can hardly see the other side of the room for smoke, even if the sun's shining. All around you are people quietly sharing each other's depression and taking comfort from the beer and smoke. Even the dogs are subdued.

Well, I must finish now—I hope everything's well with you. Try and come over sometime.

All the best,
Mark
Christiania, 10th August 1978

*I found this account of Christiania by Nicholas Saunders among cuttings I'd collected about the Freetown. His perspective is helpful; he had visited more alternative communities in the UK than anyone else when he was making his book,* Alternative England and Wales. *He brings Christiania alive with information that fills gaps in my photo essay.*

*It was written in spring 1976 after one of our trips to the Freetown and was intended for print in one of the underground newspapers that circulated in London at that time.*

### History

From its origins in the 17th century until 5 years ago, this site was an army base.

As the soldiers moved out, others moved in. At first it was pretty heavy, but once the buildings had filled up with settlers rather than dossers and lead thieves, so did the real community take shape. A new culture started to develop among people who had nothing more in common than to reject the neat Danish way of life—and the ever-so-tolerant government allowed them to stay as a 'social experiment.'

### Housing

The site is only a few minutes' walk from the city centre. As you enter, it looks like Victorian buildings and a few Nissen huts surrounding a muddy parade ground strewn with rubbish. But further in you find smaller, older buildings on both sides of a large lake whose banks have become overgrown with trees—in fact parts look like the countryside, though the city extends for miles beyond.

Indoors, some people live in squalor but many of the interiors wouldn't look out of place in *House and Garden* magazine. They've made features of the heavy wooden structures and arched windows; added balconies, skylights and even rooftop turrets. With old timber from demolition sites, they've made solid tables and partitions; some people have made complete houses from scratch.

Heating is an essential in the Danish winter—with welding equipment a range of ingenious wood-burning stoves have been made out of old oil drums and water tanks. The wood is delivered by rubbish removal contractors, who would otherwise have to cart it out of town. Glass wool insulation is practically free too, since someone discovered where the manufacturers dump reject rolls of it.

### Activities

There's a food shop selling cheap wholefood much like the English ones (except that it also sells beer and tinned dog food): an organic vegetable shop, and two other food shops. There's a bakery which produces the best quality rolls and loaves from 5am each morning; a sauna/bath house; 3 restaurants, a drinking place and several more on weekends with live music. There's also a mothers-and-babies playgroup, a kindergarten and an embryonic school; a sort of permanent jumble sale; workshops for pottery, weaving, jewellery, candlemaking, furniture repairing and a smithy. In fact, its not that clear cut—hardly a week goes by without something starting up or ending; last week the Health House reopened where people are given herbal and homeopathic remedies. And in summer especially, cafés and stalls spring up all over the place.

There's even the start of municipal services—rubbish collection supported by rates (which not everyone pays—in fact some people don't even know about).

### Arts

A couple of political theatre groups are based in Christiania but music is the big scene—the main jazz club with a turnover of more than £100,000 a year [over £600,000 today] is a focal point for the new Danish sounds—the atmosphere is amazing, you feel privileged to experience it before it hits the world. And all over Christiania you hear jam sessions late into the night.

Surprisingly, there is a lack of political or religious movements—many have moved in like missionaries and left disgusted by lack of interest.

Odd behaviour is so accepted that people who behave sanely elsewhere feel free to express the crazier aspects of their personalities. In fact it's both a place where people can be happy who would otherwise be institutionalised and a therapeutic community. Some people even helped junkies get off drugs by taking them on a long holiday to Egypt—such organised social work isn't typical, though most people are very conscious of their social responsibilities in providing an environment for those who couldn't manage outside.

### Structure

The main strength of Christiania is its lack of leaders or committees representing the whole community—the government has no one to negotiate with.

Except for rubbish collection (paid for out of a voluntary tax), each activity is a self-financed private enterprise.

Meetings are held each week for the people living in each area to decide on local issues (like whether someone can build a new place) and there's a weekly general meeting. But not many people turn up: the most important meeting in its history—to decide what to do after the government had decided to close the place—attracted less than a third of the community. I got the impression that the real decisions were made by the active people and the meetings were for those who liked to talk.

People live in a wide variety of setups—communes, families or on their own. There's an eating collective who live separately but each take it in turn to buy and prepare the evening meal.

It looks as though rules are emerging though—like already, its understood that if you're away for 3 months you can't claim back your home.

*Economy*
Dope dealing is the main income as people come to score where its relatively safe—hash only, you hardly ever come across other drugs.

There aren't any statistics, but probably one-third of the people earn money outside—from jobs, selling home-made goods, student grants, private incomes, with surprisingly few people on the dole.

The rest live off recirculated money. They work inside Christiania—earning about half what they could outside. All the activities employ a lot of people working short hours—one shop, for instance, supports 20 people. Then there are individual enterprises like mending shoes or baking cakes to sell; groups doing building work and repairing furniture—one way and another it's not hard to scrape a living there.

What is fundamental is that people do without most taken-for-granted luxuries such as hot water, so need to earn much less—a geared down economy. But it is also one based on its access to a rich city in a rich part of the world.

*Quality of life*
By modern Western standards it's a slum—most people have to go to the Christiania sauna to wash as no one has hot water and many no WCs. But what strikes me more and more is the real luxury of life there: fresh wholemeal rolls with butter and strong freshly ground coffee for breakfast is normal. All the food is best quality—the organic vegetables straight from farming communes. I never saw anyone drink instant coffee.

The work there is really worthwhile—you work with friends for friends. Your home is entirely what you've made; your skills are what you learn; your efforts are felt and appreciated. You choose your own role and do things you like doing without teachers or bosses—for most people it's their first opportunity to be responsible for themselves.

The entertainment is live—really live: you know the audience so it's like a party—and probably those playing too. Practically anything you want to get into, you'll find people to do it with—and unlike communal life it's possible to shut yourself off and avoid people too.

*Why it works*
Christiania is by no means self-sufficient—it's in a very privileged situation not only as mentioned under Economy, but by its position in the hash trade, by not paying taxes, by living rent and rates free, and having a very different society to fall back on. In fact its relations to the rest of Denmark are comparable to our relationship to Third World countries. Similarly many people in Christiania (who are enjoying this privilege also) are unaware of their position and some even believe that the whole world could be like them.

Why the lack of policing or organisation works isn't clear to me. Perhaps it's the Danish character—certainly it's difficult to believe it could happen in the UK.

But a key factor, I'm quite certain, is the constant threat from the government to close it: everyone is united in a struggle against a common enemy.

*Outside attitudes*
Though to the right-wing Christiania is an open sore that must be eradicated, and to most ordinary people it's just a slum, there are many strong supporters—including the head of Copenhagen University, along with other respected academics.

There is evidence that the crime rate went down as Christiania got going, and the cost to the taxpayer is estimated to be far less than to support all those who would have to go into institutions or on the dole.

Looked at another way, it's a concentration camp for undesirables and incapables. It has practically no amenities, no staff and you don't even have to lock them in.

Anyone can walk around Christiania. If you had done so in the closing years of the 1970s you might have noticed scenes like these in the pictures. All you needed was a Leica camera to frame these strange, beautiful, edgy moments that conjure up a past age.

Christiania's bridge, as it was in the 1970s, with its beautifully bent and twisted rails. I had spent the afternoon on the other side of the bridge trying to take a picture that would do it justice. It didn't come together, so after several hours I gave up. I decided to visit Tata in Fakirskolen. Luckily, I glanced over my shoulder as I walked along the shore to her home and there it was, a beautiful silhouette of people, some crossing the lake, others diving into the water or just chatting in the sunshine. In one moment, I'd got the picture I'd waited all afternoon for.

## KARMA AT THE LAKE

*A lot of men visit during the summer, attracted by the possibility of seeing naked women. Anna told me this short story.*

Something really funny happened to me today. Well, maybe it's not funny… I went to the long grass by the lake to sunbathe, and I was lying there without any clothes on when this guy came up and started circling me. He wanted to touch me but didn't dare, and I wasn't paying him any attention. (He'd been lying nearby, but I hadn't seen him). He didn't have any clothes on either. He hesitated for a moment, then tried to touch me. I reacted really angrily, and I think that shocked him… I know it wasn't rape but he would have fucked me if I hadn't stood my ground.

Anyway, he went back to where he'd been lying and found someone had taken all his clothes! He rushed back to ask me to help him—ha! Now the boot was on the other foot! Now it was his turn to panic!

That's real karma, isn't it? I went to a friend's house nearby and got him some trousers and some money so he could catch a bus home.

These two students had hitchhiked from Switzerland to spend a few days in Christiania. They add their beauty to the lakeside.

Rikke the bear was often to be seen around Christiania and apparently joined demonstrations and parades, though I never saw her on those occasions. Unfortunately, she became overly fond of beer. Rikke became unpredictable and was eventually taken to live out her days quietly in another part of Copenhagen— away from the temptations of the Freetown. She will be remembered for contributing to the Wild West atmosphere in Christiania in its early years.

Building up healthy levels of vitamin D.

Fire-throwing workshop.

It does look strange, knitting blankets and sweaters in the middle of summer, but I have reason to be very grateful to Tue Tuesen, seen in the foreground. He very kindly gave me the blanket he was making. I still have it—a treasured and frequently used gift.

22

Relaxing on the earthworks. Parents could catch up without worrying (too much) about their children—cars were banned in Christiania, so kids had the run of the place.

The guy with the knife told me he was serving a prison sentence but was allowed out of jail at weekends now that he was approaching his release date. He spent his free time in Christiania. If he wanted company, people would engage with him; if he wanted to sit quietly, wrapped up in his own thoughts, he was left alone.

For some, this non-institutional, community support was a vital part of recovering from the trauma of a prison sentence, or a stay in a psychiatric hospital, or a childhood blighted by violence. Christiania provided a safe haven to recover from whatever toll families and institutions inflict on the human psyche.

A moments silence between friends.

Christiania was a stage, or rather lots of stages. The road outside the general store hosted strange, impromptu shape-shifting dramas. It was a joy to catch these moments on film, but you had to be careful—if you intruded too much the actors could turn on you.

Please note: no dogs (or people) were harmed in the making of these pictures…

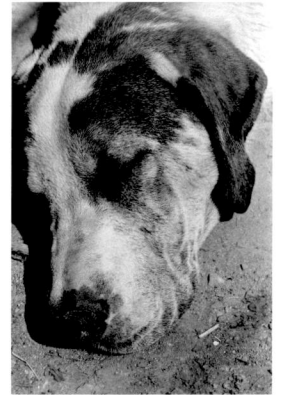

Christiania's dogs deserve a book of their own—they offered brilliant comedy on the sidelines of the Christiania stage. They had their own complicated social life and a wonderful sense of fun.

30

I recorded conversations with some of Christiania's pioneers for the original Danish edition of *Christiania* and include them in this edition (lightly edited) in sections rather than interspersed with the pictures. There are also contributions by outsiders and visitors, some critical of Christiania, some supportive. No one is indifferent.

They do not offer a coherent account of Christiania. That would surely miss the point. No one (or only the most naïve) thought that Utopia might be forged in the Freetown. Some people moved there for the opportunity to live differently, some to escape the ache of loneliness, some to hide, some to get away from their fractured past, some because they had nowhere else to go, some because they had no money, some to make money.

The Christiania tapes reflect this diversity and point to a more general sense of loss, of missing something, that many in the modern world will recognise, in spite of the great technological gains made since the industrial revolution. If one can generalise at all about the founding years of Christiania, one might *tentatively* say that here was an attempt to re-set living conditions to an earlier age, stripped of consumer excess, rich in human contact, with all the difficulties and delights that that entails.

Rather than offer a lesson for society, the Christiania of the 1970s posed a question that is just as relevant now as it was then. It held up its hand to ask if the modern world had taken a wrong turn. Did we forget what gives meaning to our lives in the rush for abundance? If the answer is yes, we have to find the solution in *our* lives, in the communities where *we* live and work. We have to find out as Andrew Marr says, 'what it means to be human'.

# VISITORS

*Visitors are not slow to pass judgement on Christiania, and it has to be said that Christianites are quite judgemental about the visitors who crowd into the Freetown every day. In the end, we all know that we are more alike than unalike but differences in lifestyle can overwhelm this simple truth. Here are some of their comments.*

'It's ugly and dirty; it smells and it should be pulled down; it's disgusting! I don't want to talk to you or anyone else—I just want to get out while I can.'

'I never thought there could be something like this in Denmark. It's not my sort of place—it looks awful, but I'm fascinated by it...'

'I have read so much about Christiania. Now I've decided to visit. It's very strange... I feel really out of place... In my world there's such poverty, not materially, but spiritually... I wanted to find out if it was different here, but nobody will talk to me.'

'People here are living off my taxes. I have a right to see how they live and I'll tell you what I think—it's disgusting. The children should be put in homes and the buildings pulled down. Christiania should be closed.'

'They should put Christianites where they put terrorists. I work from 6am. to 6pm every day, I pay 60 per cent tax, and these people can live for free. It's a terrible place. When people from Christiania come to my shop, I have to watch out in case they fill their pockets with sweets and cigarettes. They say the government removed them from the Danish law, but that's not true—they removed themselves. When the navy was here, it was a much more peaceful place, a much better place. Perhaps there are other sides to Christiania, and perhaps as a journalist you see a broader picture, but for me working here in the shop the view I get is a very bad one.'

Christianites have their own view of visitors. Lone Kellerman:[6] 'Sometimes tourists just walk into my house and look around, asking me how much I want for this piece of furniture or that picture on the wall. Really, it's too much.'

6   The Danish blues and rock singer and comedian who died in 2005

*Imagine a large smoke-filled room, loud music, dogs and pushers tripping over themselves and Knud and I sitting at a wooden table in the middle of it all. He talked out of the side of his mouth in a rich southern American drawl. He parodied the mannerisms of a corrupt politician beautifully. Movie posters tell us that Sean Connery is James Bond. By the same token, Knud is Ruler of the World.*

*How would you describe Christiania?*

It's a question of reality—a pressure from the rainbow—the strength of my voice and what I'm saying. My first impression of Christiania, way back in 1976, was of the Third World, like India or Africa. All the poor people are our natural allies. This is our revolution. But we don't want violence. We tell everyone, 'Take it easy, do it your own way, in your own time.' In Christiania we do it here and now—this means tomorrow.

This is Knud, painter and artist by first profession, speaking to the world as Ruler of the World, from Fælleskøkkenet café in Christiania, Tuesday, 2nd September, I mean 1st February, at about seven o'clock GMT. This is recording everything I say, and the more clearly and closely I speak, the louder the world can hear, and it's important the world hears it… I speak in a soft voice, as you can hear. I'm forty. I told you I'm a driver and painter by profession, but I'm very careful. As a driver I never take a chance. Nor do I as a painter, because it's poisonous—the paint, I mean. I get it all over my hands, on my face even, and on my body, but I don't eat it. I could probably survive if I did—I would survive—but why should I eat it? It's not going to do me any good.

*What is the first law you will make as Ruler of the World?*

Well, I'll go and live in a place that was formerly the emperor's palace. The first law would be: Take it easy—everybody, take it easy. Do the things you want to do. Be pleasant, be tolerant. Avoid violence. Right now, I'm speaking to the entire world, including South Africa, all the places where war is about to break out. I mean Mozambique, Angola, Ethiopia, the Middle East (money, money)!

*Do you see yourself adopting Kissinger's approach?*

Yes, yes, very much, but in a completely different way. Yes, indeed, but I don't want to make his mistakes. Well, he's out now, isn't he, and I'm in. And of course, I want to stay on for some time.

*Twenty years?*

No. Fourteen days. Then we'll hold a common meeting in Christiania, we'll elect our own government and install it officially in the Grey Hall with a big celebration. This will enable the hippies to speak with the Establishment. We don't intend to bring down the Establishment. We're just going to paint a lot of grey men and concrete buildings in bright colours.

*Could you work with the UN?*

Of course, of course. We'll have to specify on what terms we're willing to appear. I'm willing to make two speeches, one prepared and one impromptu. I'll even dance, of course, if I can be brought in alive and taken away alive… or just taken in alive.

I welcome suggestions on how I'm going to get there, but I require tight security. Personally, I find rule number one for the state is security. An elephant bears its child in the jungle, it's built for the jungle, but humans are weak. I could turn around the wrong way and bash my head or my arm. In Christiania we are built more for the jungle. I had a letter from a girlfriend, a musician. She went to Bangladesh and wrote to me from Dacca. (She'd never been to Christiania, she only knows it from my description.) But she wrote: 'Dear Knud, This is such a low and poor country, just like Christiania. If there was a major world disaster, I think you'd survive.'

She's thirty-eight, a lover, a mistress. We helped lever each other out of our marriages four years ago. After that we were friends, still a bit in love. I'm a bit in love with a lot of girls. That doesn't mean I sleep with all of them. That would be too much for me. When I'm sexually in love, it's a major thing for me. It influences all my other actions. *Shall we fire this piece of Afghan? We need a chillum…* My personal theory about sex is influenced by Indian art and African love stories. I'm not interested in the sexual behaviour of the members of my government—if they have other ways of feeling and thinking, that's fine with me.
*What do you think Christiania's role in the world is?*

To make the world behave itself, Shall we fire this chillum? I don't have any matches.

*And the world's relationship to Christiania?*

To give us a chance. For two weeks. Personally, I live day by day. To me two weeks is a long way off. Today there's sunshine, and in the northern province of Christiania where I live all the small flowers have come out… I just gave away all my private belongings. Money, I have, but I also give it away—sometimes very fast, sometimes more slowly. According to my own records, every year I'm one of the ten cheapest inhabitants in Christiania, because I do work that I don't charge for. I should be on the economic council, but I am just Ruler of the World.

I will make you Minister of Foreign Affairs, Mark. You'll have to go to New York sometimes, make some speeches, fly back and forth—but you'll be paid for it.

Besides being Ruler of the World, I may have to be Prime Minister of Denmark. I can take on that job as well. I may even have time for three jobs. I could also handle a job as a professor at the academy. That would be my way of relaxing.

I'm a free man appointed by you, the people. I live in the streets, I come from the streets, but the policies we're going to bring in will affect where I live in future.

There has never been a government in history more open to negotiation than this one. We stand for non-violence and the only power we have is spiritual power and human power, just like Christiania, which has existed for six and a half years on a voluntary basis, a planetary basis, exposed to violence and hatred from the Danish bourgeoisie. These attacks are based on non-facts, on things never seen, turned into newspaper articles that have an impact on public opinion in Denmark. All the criticism I've seen about Christiania comes from not knowing what it is. They don't know what they're talking about. If they see Christiania as it really is, they will accept it, and it won't be closed by the Danish government.

*Christiania has attracted support from unexpected quarters. It's a community without laws, and yet many lawyers support it; there's no social welfare system, and yet many social workers support it; there's no government, and yet some ministers support it; it's an unplanned community, and yet many town planners support it.*

*What appeals to these professionals is the attempt by ordinary people to create their own environment and culture. Christiania has provided an extraordinary opportunity, unheard of in Western Europe since the industrial revolution and the growth of powerful central governments, to rediscover how a community can develop without formal structures. Of course, Christiania is gradually being drawn back into 'the system', at the bidding of both the government and of many Christianites themselves.*

*Steen Eiler Rasmussen was, until he retired, Chief Town Planner for Copenhagen. At the time of our conversation, the Supreme Court was about to pass judgement on the future of Christiania.*

*I asked what he felt about this community that evolves to suit its own social needs.*

I think it's the most encouraging thing I have seen in my life. What's wonderful is that you have a place that brings out the creative side of people. There are many people living there who can't live anywhere else—who can't live in society.

I once planned a suburb of Copenhagen as well as I possibly could, providing as many facilities as possible for the people living there. It was for very poor people, and I built playgrounds, schools, everything. But according to the police, the area has the highest crime rate in the city. Sometimes even the youth clubs I designed get completely wrecked by the youths who use them. What I learnt from that place and from Christiania was that if you create a total environment for people, they are never satisfied. The lesson is that you should provide space for playgrounds, for example, and provide children with materials to make the things that suit the games they want to play. Where I adopted this approach, it worked well.

Christiania proves that if you give people who aren't accepted by society a chance to live their own life, something positive comes out of it.

When criminals come out of prison and feel unwanted, they just smash the place up. Britain used to send convicts to Australia, and look what happened. Sydney was built by criminals, just ordinary people. They weren't in jail, but they couldn't escape—there was the sea on one side and the bush on the other. But they built a society.

The question that Christiania raises is: who really owns the place? Is it the Ministry of Defence, which has the title deeds, or the people that use it? And that's what Parliament has to decide. The lawyers argue that Christiania has a certain right to it, because they have made use of the area. That's the English way, the pragmatic way. The English legal system relates to the way people want to live. The German legal system is more theoretical. Fortunately, Denmark is more like Britain in this respect. The Germans have their strict rules for everything. The English and Danish do things in a practical way.

I think the government have tried to help Christiania as much as they can. The real enemies are the police. I don't know why they are so against Christiania. They probably want to justify their own existence by doing something. When Christiania reached an agreement with the government and was given 'social experiment' status, the occupants wanted to make contact with the police and cooperate with them, but the police would never speak to them. Of course, by police I mean the Uro Patrol [Uropatruljen was the notorious Danish riot squad, feared for its brutal behaviour and irregular methods. It operated between 1965 and 2001, and mainly dealt with drug trafficking, particularly in squatter communities].

There should actually be a patrol to take action against *them*—they are creating trouble, not stopping it. They should be made to respect people in Christiania in the same way that they respect citizens living outside. I think the government should draw up another contract with Christiania—an extension of the previous one. If there was a formal contract the police wouldn't be able to act in the way they do.

*It seems strange to me that a town planner should support Christiania—an unplanned community.*

No, I believe people should learn from nature and from human nature. You shouldn't try to make human nature adhere to some kind of theory.

# PER AND VIBEKE

*Any journalist who goes to Christiania ends up talking to Per and Vibeke. I was no exception. Alex and his girlfriend, Pernille, also looked in; he added his views, while Pernille regarded us all with disdain (she became a close friend later on when we got to know each other).*

*I did not really get to know Per and Vibeke until much later. I used to call in to see them and tell them about my adventures in Christiania. Later, I stayed with them and had a wonderful time. They had that special (and, in Christiania, unusual) ability needed to negotiate with politicians, though it earned them distrust in some quarters.*

*Christiania is called a Freetown, but that perhaps is the most difficult thing for an outsider to understand. Could you explain how a community of one thousand people and six hundred dogs functions? Is it anarchy?*

Per: I've never described it as anarchy… we wouldn't use such a simple definition, because Christiania is something unique. It's a place where people have to be more aware, not dependent on the community outside.

We're not here just to have a good time together. We're here to try to create conditions that are meaningful in a wider sense. I look upon Christiania as a sort of miracle in the middle of a capitalist system. A community based on use rather than ownership. Practice comes before theory here.

One big problem is that we have so many social casualties. I think that's because these people have lost their role in society. They don't have to fight for their own lives—they get social security anyway. I've talked to three of these people today, two from the psychiatric hospital, and one from here, and they all have the same problem—they feel that they don't have a place in society. In Christiania nobody is forced to decide what to do with their lives so although they still have a problem here, it's of a different kind.

*The propaganda for Christiania gives the impression that it's not a capitalistic community, whereas I find that in many ways it's very close to right-wing philosophy—free enterprise, low tax, everybody doing their own thing…*

Per: Whereas a left-wing policy would be heavy taxation, central bureaucracy and the state organising the welfare of the community? Well, that can't work here, because people hate authority. But the major difference between capitalism and Christiania is that people here don't work for a 'boss'.

*Well, that brings us back to where we started—you said that you did not describe this as anarchy.*

Per: Yes, but Christiania does have some ideals close to the spirit of anarchy. We've created a situation here where you're free to do things in your own way, on your own terms. You have to accept that you're part of a community and you mustn't destroy that community. It's essential that people coming here have the feeling that they have a chance to do things. And that's still a kind of freedom, even if you have to take the community into consideration.

Vibeke: You can see this when you build your own home. You have to do it on your own, but you must also plan it with your neighbours. Now Christiania is divided into districts because you can't talk to a thousand people, but you can talk to the people in your own neighbourhood.

*Do you see a municipal structure evolving in Christiania as it becomes more established? Will it function more like Copenhagen?*

Per: Yes, I think so—in some respects. There are already organised groups, like the people who collect the rubbish, and those running the shops and the restaurants.

*What forms do the meetings take? The ones I've been to have been quite unusual. Anybody at all is allowed to talk and is always listened to sympathetically; and they can go on and on and on as long as they want. How are decisions actually made?*

Per: Mostly these meetings take place because there is a practical problem to solve. If it's a big problem, we have to discuss it first at district meetings. Then the district meetings take their decisions to a common meeting. Eventually a decision is reached by finding some kind of compromise.

Alex: Yes, it's done in a democratic way, but there's a high level of apathy so only a small number of people actually participate. It's really quite a small group that takes decisions. You have to be very strong to make your opinions heard.

*What kind of issues are brought up at the big meetings?*

Per: The major problem now is all the summer visitors, because they cause a lot of trouble. We've had lots of discussions about this, about

45

whether we should let them come in and stay. We do like people to come and support us in our struggle for survival, but at the same time they cause us practical problems. You may be able to accommodate a hundred people in the 'sleep-ins', but if you do that, they expect to be able to stay permanently. Last year the sleep-ins didn't work at all well, so we decided that we're not obliged to take in all these summer visitors coming to Copenhagen. If people are seriously interested and want to help, then they will find some Christianites to stay with, but everyone else should be referred to a tourist campsite.

Another problem is caused by people from town, who can't find a job and are having a rough time, the so-called social losers. Should Christiania provide an alternative to Copenhagen's organised social welfare system? We had to say that we couldn't take on all these problems, they are not ours. At the same time, we feel that this goes against the principle that anyone should be allowed to come here. So that is something we have discussed a great deal. We don't impose strict rules or regulations—in the meetings we try instead to encourage a certain attitude.

*And at a recent meeting, you discussed the question of guns, didn't you?*

Per: Well, we proposed setting aside a place where people could practise shooting. A guy who was using a gun and acting aggressively was told that he couldn't behave like that, because it affected the entire community and threatened our mutual survival. He agreed—that's the kind of solution Christiania finds. This is the way things have functioned for the past few years. The question is whether this approach will continue to work.

*What were your first impressions of Christiania, when you came here?*

Per: My first impression was that it was an enormous place with a lot of possibilities. When we came here most of the houses were vacant, we could take what we wanted. My first thought was that we really had an opportunity to see how people acted when they had the chance to do things on their own. How would they organise things? That was my first interest in Christiania.

Vibeke: Well, for me it was more a question of finding a place to live in a more viable way with other people.

*If Christiania could have been taken over in an orderly, progressive way from the start, do you think it would have made a lot of difference to the way it developed?*

Per: The whole thing started up so spontaneously; you had a lot of different people with different viewpoints, trying to find ways to organise themselves, which meant that you built up a sort of tolerance. You were united in your need to survive, because of the threat from outside, and it became essential for you to be part of Christiania—to identify yourself as a Christianite. On the other hand, I feel that Christiania might have developed in a better way if our situation had been truly accepted by the authorities when they decided that the Freetown should be a social experiment. The threat has been never-ending, it has gone too far. People feel too insecure about their situation here.

*This threat from 'outside' creates an artificial feeling of solidarity, though. When there is the possibility of closure by the government there is a tremendous spirit of cooperation and it seems to me Christiania has become dependent on this pressure from the outside world to reconcile differences between the people here. Politicians often pretend their country is nearly at war to generate this same feeling…*

Per: Well, you are asking for a perfect world—a world without threats. The question is: are we going to survive or is the capitalist system going to survive?

*Ove came by appointment to my room, exactly on time. 'I've decided not to worry about my English'—which was excellent—'it's your job to correct it. I'm just going to tell you my story. Then you do what you want with it.' I turned the tape recorder on, and he talked. Even if I'd wanted to ask questions, I wouldn't have had a chance—there was hardly time to turn the tape over. When he finished, he got up, wished me well and left.*

In the winter of 1971, I was living in the country, completely alone, working as a teacher. One morning I woke to find that there had been a heavy fall of snow—it was so cold my moped wouldn't start. I had no neighbours so I had a long walk to a telephone box to tell the school that I couldn't go to work that day. When I came to the place where the telephone box should have been, I found it had been removed. I've never felt so alone, so completely cut off from the world. I decided to return to Copenhagen to see my girlfriend. We'd read about Christiania, so we decided to have a look and see what it was all about. When we arrived, Christiania was covered in virgin snow. It looked beautiful. We were walking around when I noticed a child throwing stones at the windows of a small building. I dashed over to stop him, having no idea that a few months later I would be standing there with a glass cutter repairing each window he had smashed and turning that building into the Indkøbscentralen (the general store…)

It was terribly cold and it felt a bit eerie standing there (a small black dog with a bleeding foot had followed us everywhere so we could see exactly where we'd been), but I was struck more and more forcibly by the possibilities in Christiania. There were just a few signs of other inhabitants. '007 was here', I read on one wall. Suddenly I decided to move in. It was crazy but I started looking for a house straight away. We were very choosy, checking how the sun would come up in each room. It was a fantastic feeling. Eventually, we chose Mælkebøtten because the houses there were in very good condition; they even had paraffin in the fuel tanks—you just had to put a match to the burner. We decided to move into No. 7.

We discussed everything, from how many people should live there to how we should do up the room. And then we went home, I grabbed the phone and rang a friend, who I'd met in a commune, and I said to him, 'This place is fantastic! You should move with us to Christiania—there's a whole house we can have; we'll create something together.' He said, 'Yes, yes, I'll be there in two hours.' He hadn't seen it; he knew nothing about it; he only had our word. Two hours later he was there, with another friend, and we were sitting on the floor making plans. We decided to go and collect our mattresses, a stove, candles and a few

other things in a car. The next morning, we drove back out here, parked outside the house and started carrying our stuff in. But another guy had already moved in with some of his things. We almost cried. He'd moved in just a couple of hours before. We tried to explain how we felt about it, how we really wanted the house. We were discussing it in a friendly way when another guy, Per Løvetand, came in. It turned out he also had plans for our house, so now there were three groups, all trying to discuss it politely but all really wanting it. Then suddenly a fourth guy arrived—Kjeld, who was already living in No. 2 —and he tried to manage the negotiations.

After a while he said that we could come and have a look at his house—there was a big room next to the one he was sharing with his brother. We decided it would be fantastic to make a communal room out of it—we could leave the shelves as they were, put our books on them, we could make space for a workshop . . . As we were talking it over, we agreed to move in together—and that's what we did. So we had our first evening in Christiania, with only a paraffin lamp, some candles, the old stove, and a few mattresses in the room.

We found that we could live on 200 Kr. a month, but we couldn't afford to keep the oil stove burning all night, so we'd get up early. We started to work, and our place quickly became the focal point of Mælkebøtten.

We met a lot of people in a very short time. It was our group that came up with the idea of common meetings—we put up big posters on the kitchen windows saying 'COMMON MEETING every Monday at 19.30', with the words 'representative democracy is bad and society is corrupt' written underneath.

We worked very hard, and after two or three weeks I knew about two hundred people by name. It was such a nice feeling, walking down the street—all the time there would be people saying, 'Hi, Ove, we're really making it happen', 'Hi, Ove, great meeting yesterday!'. Such a change after living alone! Now I felt I was a member of a community. It was a fantastic life—you saw people moving in with all their belongings on carts. A restaurant had been set up too, so everybody went there to eat.

At the common meetings we would discuss what we should do about getting rid of the rubbish, connecting to water and electricity, and things like that. At that time, Kjeld was one of the self-appointed group trying to run things, but our group believed that the common meetings were where decisions should be made. In the end his group fell apart because the common meetings undermined their work. People didn't want them to run things over their heads.

One evening Kjeld and I were talking about these issues, and he said, 'But what about all your ideals? You've got to prove they work.'

So we decided to open a shop, owned by the community. The people working there would be paid by the hour. We had a common problem in getting food, paraffin and other stuff in Christiania, so why not solve it communally? We found that house with the twenty-two windows down there—an old smithy—and we cleaned it up and formed an 'economy group' at the common meeting. We had no initial capital, so we decided to do a collection. We sat by the door of Multimedia House, where a kind of music festival was taking place, and asked people to contribute 1 or 2 Kr. to start up a community shop. We ended up with about 125 Kr. (£12.50). The idea was to start by selling paraffin. We got in contact with different companies and it was amazing to see all the company reps coming out here with their briefcases, discussing how many litres Christiania needed. We gave them an idea of how many people and how many houses there were in total—it was quite a lot. So, we talked to Mobil Oil, because we wanted to have a tank so that people could come and fill their own containers. We had a draft contract drawn up and discussed it at the common meeting. At first, people thought it was a very good idea, but then started to get too idealistic, saying that we had to order it from Libya or another socialist country, direct, not through an oil company, and so our work was sabotaged. But we took it in our stride and opened 'Indkøbscentralen' on 7th January 1972. We've kept it open every day of the year ever since, except when we closed for spring cleaning. On the first day we sold 94 Kr. worth of paraffin, and it went on from there.

We became good friends with the head of the Defence Ministry's Building Department, Frode Christensen, and he arranged for electricity to be installed. He also drew up a permit allowing us to put up a fuel tank—it was the first official document drawn up by the 'other side', the authorities, accepting that we existed.

The shop went from strength to strength. Another guy came to work with us. He had some retail experience, so knew how to get in touch with wholesalers. He went to a phone box and ordered toilet paper and all sorts of other stuff we needed.

The reason I moved out of Christiania? I left when I realised that people always have to change. When they have learnt something, they have to move on and discover new things—at least I have to. So, I finished at Indkøbscentralen and started working on a film about Christiania.

When I first moved into Christiania, I could see the horizon—but after a while that horizon changed because they started to build the Hotel Scandinavia. That change got into the view from my window, and it made me see that things were happening outside. Suddenly I realised that they'd built that hotel on another old military camp and something similar might happen to Christiania. I realised how redevelopment was going directly against the interests and ideas of the citizens living in Christianshavn (the district of Copenhagen in which Christiania lies). And I thought that we should do something about it, but I didn't have the self-confidence to take the initiative. Then I discovered that the locals had set up an organisation, and I got more and more involved in it. Meanwhile in Christiania, the thinking was that the Freetown was enough by itself—it was self-sufficient in a way—so why try to solve the problems of the rest of Denmark? The solution was to form other communities like Christiania—everybody should do it—which would all eventually unite and work together. I could see that this meant turning our backs on life outside, turning our eyes and our consciousness away from what was happening. A very strong community had developed in our house by this time, but I felt contradictions within myself and it felt natural for me to move away.

Christiania goes round in circles because everyone wants to learn from their own experience, not from other people. I felt that I wanted to get out to work with new people again. I like people, and I believe in people.

I wanted a job, and I got one in a big shipyard as a welder. I never regretted it and when I left Christiania, it was on good terms. Christiania fulfils a need, and it's absolutely clear that however rotten you consider Fredens Ark to be, for example, the fact is, people still live there, and this must be because they don't want to, or can't, live anywhere else. They could live in an institution, but they choose to live there, and you have to respect their choice. So I moved out of Christiania with a smile. We could say goodbye over a few beers—it really was okay because I was leaving without any hard feelings.

# ANTI-PLANNING — KAI LEMBURG

*Kai Lemberg was an economist and town planner, and the General Planning Director of Copenhagen from 1968 to 1987.*

I take the idea of participation in planning very seriously—as a necessity in fact, because planning must relate to the way people want to live. We normally think of planning as experts giving technical information to citizens, teaching them how to make the best use of an area. But that is only one side of it. The other side is people deciding how to live for themselves and taking responsibility for their environment. And that's why I value Christiania—it's a successful example of anti-planning.

*Do you see a negative side to anti-planning in Christiania?*

Certainly. The physical condition of many houses is unsatisfactory, particularly the sanitation, insulation and fire precautions.

But it's very difficult to improve these things when the relationship be¬tween the authorities and the inhabitants is as bad as it is, and when the future is so uncertain that people are reluctant to make an investment in their buildings.

But, generally, I think it's a very good idea to try and let people live in this way. Traditional social policy suffers from institutional inflexibility. Christiania is not the solution to all of society's problems, but it's a solution for some people. It seems to work well for runaway children, for example.

I'm sure that Britain's cities could use Christianias. It's definitely a phenomenon of big cities. You can't put Christiania on a desert island— there has to be the possibility of work nearby and facilities that are only available in cities.

In fact, there is considerable interest abroad. At a committee in Washington where I was speaking on social welfare policy and planning with other European planners, there was more interest in Christiania than anything else. You may be interested to read a report I prepared for the OECD: Urban Environment Group on Management of Publicly Owned Land.

*The following is an extract from this paper by Kai Lemberg:*

Christiania was started by people taking the law into their own hands, not respecting property and prohibitions; disrespectful youngsters not (fully) paying for their use of the buildings or for water and electricity. A belief developed that disorder, immorality and subversive conduct were prevalent there. This was shocking to many ordinary citizens, especially older people and the middle classes, in rural areas and small towns.

Many consider Christiania a threat to law and order and have accused the Chris¬tianites of violating the law and disregarding decisions made by the Folketing (the Danish Parliament), thus placing themselves outside the general community and threatening democracy. In addition, their criminal activities are said to pose a risk to society, especially the black market in hash. Christiania is also a hiding place for wanted criminals and runaway children and has unacceptably low housing standards. Continued acceptance of this sort of alternative settlement that breaks all the rules might have an infectious effect, stimulating others to disrespect property rights and the rule of law.

An official report presented by the Copenhagen Police Director to the Ministry of Justice in October 1975 described Christiania as the largest centre for drug trafficking in Copenhagen, and pointed out that during the first nine months of 1975, the Uro Patrol made 167 arrests in connection with drugs offences. Furthermore, violence and theft were reported to be rife in the area, with increasing numbers of assaults and robberies. Other police officials claimed in newspaper articles that Christiania was the largest centre for the receipt of stolen goods in Denmark and that 27.9 per cent of the inhabitants were known criminals.

Other opponents of Christiania resented the fact that the Christianites used the area and the buildings, as well as water and electricity, practically without charge, and that the state was paying for repairs, improvements and social welfare. They believed that the Christianites were obstruc¬ting the proper and more economically viable use of the area, for example the planned new housing, public institutions and parkland.

To sum up, the main arguments put forward against Christiania are:
1) A society based on the rule of law cannot allow people to take the law into their own hands.
2) It is wrong that some people sponge on society by not paying for water and electricity.
3) The antisocial character of Christiania attracts and fosters dangerous social groups, such as drug addicts and criminals.
4) In parts of Christiania, the housing conditions are unacceptable for reasons of health and fire risk.
5) Children living in Christiania are exposed to moral risks, criminality and drugs.
6) Left-wing political groups are using Christiania for their subversive activities.

Many politicians, organisations and individuals have defended the existence of Christiania. Several medical spokespeople, including the

City Officer for Health, say that it does not to represent any substantial risk to health. Housing conditions are admittedly poor in some cases but still better than in some older parts of Copenhagen or the wooden barracks for homeless people to which many Christianites would be directed in a rehousing programme after an eviction. The fire risks are high, but they are worse in other areas of Copenhagen.

The number of serious drug addicts in Christiania is very small— hard narcotics are generally kept out, though hashish is used by many people and sold by some. The real drug trafficking in Copenhagen is concentrated outside Christiania, in Inner Nørrebro and Inner Vesterbro. The Director for Child and Youth Welfare in Copenhagen has pointed out that runaway children are not arriving in Christiania and then becoming drug addicts and criminals. Rather, they already have problems before they arrive. By being accepted in Christiania, and having no unreasonable expectations imposed on them, they have a much better chance of recovery than in the tougher surroundings they have come from, where they often succumb to mental health problems, crime or prostitution (there is no prostitution in Christiania). Through the contacts developed with people in Christiania, the Child and Youth Welfare Directorate has motivated 300-400 children to leave the Freetown and start a normal life.

The aforementioned report on alleged criminality in Christiania by the Copenhagen Police Director has been severely criticised by sociologists, criminologists and social workers as being one-sided and misleading, as it omits to compare the figures for Christiania with those of other parts of Copenhagen and Denmark. Statistics show that criminality in Christiania is at much the same level as elsewhere in the country—and much lower than in the Inner Nørrebro and Inner Vesterbro areas of Copenhagen… Most recorded criminal activities in Christiania are connected with the sale or use of hash, but the police make no distinction between hash and hard narcotics. A report published by the University of Copenhagen reveals low levels of serious crime in Christiania.

The Freetown's supporters claim that the Christianites have not damaged the buildings; in fact, they have started repairing and improving them. Most of the damage was done before their arrival, by scrap metal dealers and vandals while the area was left empty and unprotected.

Another objection to the closure of the settlement is that there is no final and detailed town plan for the future use of the area; it will be two or three years before the area is prepared for another use. Furthermore, no adequate plans for rehousing the inhabitants have been presented. Offers of individual rehousing in vacant flats, barracks, rented rooms or even prisons will not be a solution, as this option does not take into account the sense of community and the alternative type of settlement that Christiania provides.

Some organisations—including the Danish Architects' Association and the Association of Town Planners—have defended Christiania's continued existence as a way of guaranteeing the conservation of this beautiful landscape, and protecting the many houses worthy of preservation. They fear that eviction would pave the way for the large-scale construc¬tion of visually intrusive buildings on the site.

As for the complaints regarding lack of payments for elec¬tricity and water supply, Christiania's defenders claim this is of only marginal importance compared with the fraud and tax evasion that go on elsewhere.

An analysis carried out by an academic at the Danish Technical High School comparing the costs of clearing and preserving the site found that clearances would, during 1976-80, cost the state some 19 million Kr. (£1,900,000) and the city some 29 million Kr. (£2,900,000) more than preservation, with social reintegration, criminal care, child and youth welfare and facilities for drug addicts accounting for the greatest expenditure. The main costs of preservation would be refurbishment and maintenance of the area and the buildings.

The most important part of the argument in favour of Christiania, however, is the view of the settlement as a positive phenomenon. Left-wing and centre politicians, and many intellectuals, have publicly supported it as a valuable human and social experiment, identifying it as an alternative to a competitive market economy based on increasing material consumption. They highlight the importance of socio-psychological experiments, where personal fellowship and unconditional acceptance, neighbourhood democracy without leaders, and a life based on low material requirements, low-energy and low-pollution techniques, recycling and zero-growth are key values. This sort of community, it is claimed, gives the social losers and the weak the chance of a meaningful and active life on their own terms, in a way that is impossible in ordinary urban environments or in traditional institutions.

The Danish tradition of tolerance and experiment encourages acceptance of alternative lifestyles, and allows a wide margin for possible failures and mistakes.

*The ideological conflict underlying the christiania case*

Within the larger contexts of town planning in city, regional and national policy, Christiania seems to have attracted a disproportionate amount of public attention. This is partly due to the fact that Christiania symbolises a broader clash between contrasting political and moral attitudes. It's also true that colourful protest movements have generally received a wide coverage in the Danish media.

The Freetown of Christiania may be considered an offshoot of the late 60s youth rebellion, with elements of popular protest against traditional town planning, institutional inflexi¬bility and the belief that economic growth is the overall goal.

Sociologists and psychologists analysing Christiania point to the fact that happy and satisfied people have a sort of 'psychic surplus', which allows space for tolerance and acceptance of the strange and the unusual. Confused and dissatisfied people, on the other hand, generally have lower tolerance thresholds. Their suppressed anxiety tends to lead to aggression and hate, often directed against some scapegoat. Christiania is an outstanding scapegoat.

The period of extraordinary economic growth during the 1960s undoubtedly increased production, consumption and material welfare, but this material progress was, to a large extent, offset by damage to the environment, increasing pollution, noise, stress and mental health problems. These factors combined to produce a lack of human contact and feelings of rootlessness, exacerbated, in turn, by the breakdown of traditional norms and values.

Then came the economic and social problems of the 1970s, when inflationary growth was followed by a period of 'stagflation', with high unemployment and insecurity, rising taxes and rents, and cuts to social services and education.

The way people react to these changes depends on their position in the production process, in the labour market and on their personal status and power. In the debate over Christiania, it has often been stated that objective and factual arguments, not emotions and opinions, should steer the discus¬sion and influence decisions, as if the problem were primarily a matter of information, analysis and finding the optimal technical and legal solutions. But in fact, it is really above all a question of deciding which are the fundamental objectives for urban development and finding effective ways to reintegrate what Christiania calls 'social losers' into society. As a result, Christiania is—and must be—a question of emotions and opinions. There is no such thing as a perfect solution to the issues it raises.

One type of inward-oriented reaction to these changes is characterised by a shift in values; inner, emotional wellbeing becomes more important than material progress. People may try to escape the reality of their situation through the use of drugs, or they may develop religious feelings, or a nostalgic longing for a primitive or different life.

Others may have a more outward-looking way of dealing with their personal problems, criticising society and authorities, seeking active greater self-development, meaningful work (instead of just 'employment'), two-way communication and participation in public planning and decision-making.

Both these reactions are, I believe, to be found in Christiania.

Many of the opponents of Christiania, strengthened by the swing to the political right in the last few years, have a self-protecting attitude. They seek security through income, efficient education, conformity to traditional ideals and defence of the old values and norms. They generally feel anger towards those who reject the old values. It is a backlash ideology with low tolerance thresholds.

In such an ideological confrontation, it is not surprising that a more balanced conception of conflict and disagreement as logical products of a dynamic society gives way to absolute attitudes and fixed positions.

In terms of physical planning, Christiania may be considered as an example of a spontaneous 'anti-planning' movement, which disregards many existing laws and regulations. This movement has developed in Christiania in the framework of poor housing standards and very poor social services, but with a high degree of direct personal contact, mutual help within the community and personal development and self-realisation.

## BEHIND CLOSED DOORS

Here are just a few of the rooms in Christiania, alive with light and colour. One of the great Danish exports is *hygge*, which I understand to mean a kind of sophisticated cosiness. Christiania developed its own take on that style, what might be called Hippy Hygge.

Look at these pictures quietly and you'll hear the echo of laughter and wonderful conversations in the warm glow of candlelight (from candles made by Michael, of course).

If this sounds a bit too romantic, the last picture in this section shows what happened if the Uro Patrol (*uro* means unrest) invited themselves in for a visit.

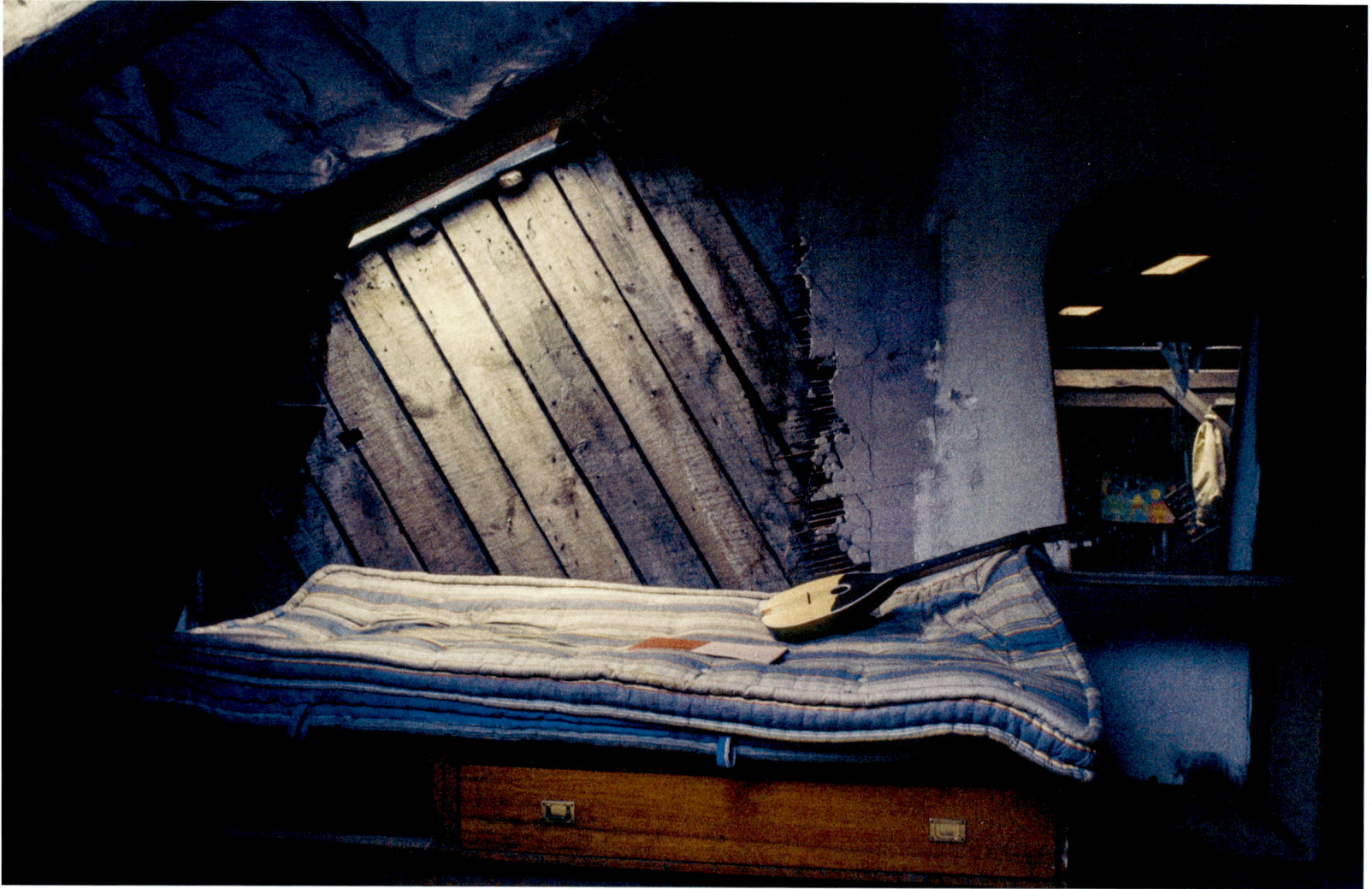

This was one of the rooms the Uro Patrol pulled apart in their search for drugs. The Uro Patrol, officially called the Uropatruljen, was the notorious Danish riot squad, feared for its brutal behaviour and irregular methods. It operated between 1965 and 2001, and mainly dealt with drug trafficking, particularly in squatter communities.

They were as much a part of Christiania as the hash dealers and constituted, throughout the time I was making this book, an enemy that brought Christianites together in common cause. For all the violence they perpetrated on the Freetown, they had only a marginal effect on the sale of hash.

Here is a glimpse of daily life in Christiania. People waking up, getting ready for work, cooking and bringing up children. It was a privilege to share and photograph these personal moments. I was grateful at the time; I'm even more grateful now that I can share them again after all these years.

The technology and conventions of photography give a particular look to each generation's images. I was using film at the edge of its capacity, pushing it to the limits of its sensitivity so that I could use natural light. It would be a very different book if it was made now with digital cameras. They effortlessly capture pictures in impossibly low light with a sharpness and plasticity that has a special beauty. But I think Tri-X[7] and Kodak Recording Film[8] were the right medium to present Christiania as it was in the 1970s.

Sometimes an old photograph, or an anniversary, will remind you that you are not the person you once were. Without noticing it, you have travelled a great distance; the values you held to, the opinions you defended, no longer ring true. Sometimes we continue to defend them, even when we know they have lost their meaning. The Quakers (and they should know) coined the expression 'Inspiration, organisation, fossilisation'. It can apply to communities and to us as individuals, and points to our tendency to keep trying to manage the ever-changing challenges life throws at us with outdated attitudes and beliefs.

We all need to be shaken *and* stirred so we don't end up holding on to assumptions that are no longer appropriate. Christiania, which did more than its fair share of shaking and stirring Danish society—and me—in the period this book covers, might ask what kind of role (if any) it should adopt at the beginning of its next half-century.

This also raises the question: what happened to the 1960s counterculture? Here is an example of a movement that really did travel a great distance. The counterculture spawned the contemporary environmental movement, which had at its heart a new perception of the world and our place in it. It brought art, science and enlightened politics together to explore a new impulse—sustainable development: development that meets the needs of the present without compromising the ability of future generations to meet theirs. The counterculture and Christiania show that we do have the power to change society. Everything starts with a few people; no one knows what will catch on in the wider world and deflect the course of history.

---

7   Kodak Tri-X was a popular black and white film used by photojournalists from the 1960s. Its sales declined as colour film became popular. Tri-X has all but fallen out of use in newspaper journalism but it is still used by a small group of documentary photographers. The emulsion has been re-engineered to use less silver and the images it produces now have a different character.

8   Kodak Recording Film 2475 was the most sensitive film available in the 1970s. It was produced for police surveillance until 2000. It had an extended red sensitivity (all the better to see you under tungsten light) and was coated on a maddingly curly Estar base. I was always careful not to leave the film boxes behind, as the instructions were written for police photographers and might have raised all kinds of suspicions.

The pictures on this page and the following eight pages are all taken in Den Kosmiske Blomst, the first place I lived when I visited Christiania. They are included here with huge thanks to one and all for the kindness I was shown.

74

Mette and Torsten just after the birth of their baby boy. See
page 92 to read about their life together.

Winter 1977.

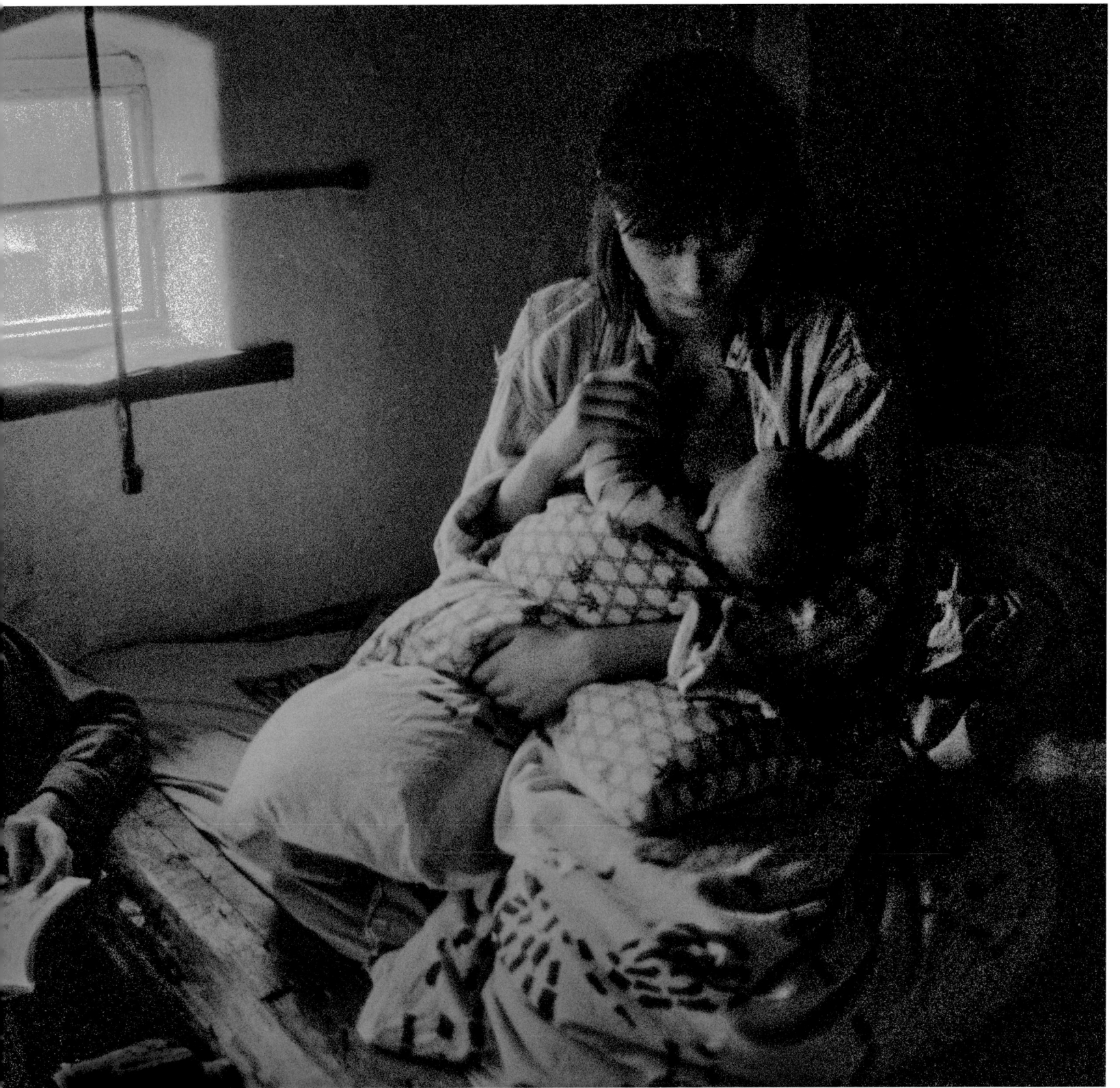

Patrick and Annetta.

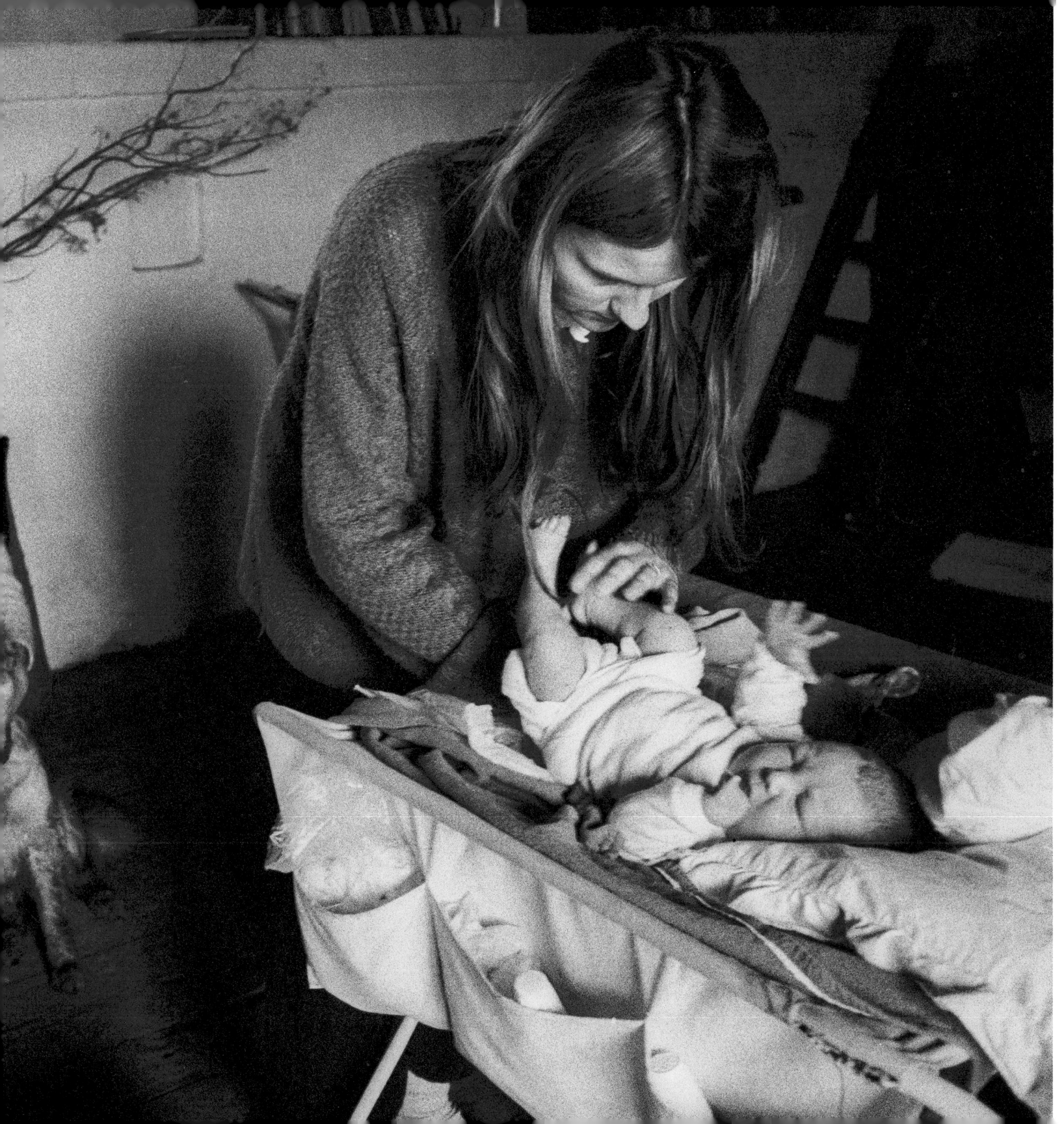

Tommy and Marianna.

Ebba and Søren.

Ouch… Kim and Bo, or Bo and Kim at the Dome home.

Ouch again... There must be some kind of evolutionary advantage to this sort of behaviour. Admiring glances from Putte, standing in the background, might offer a clue.

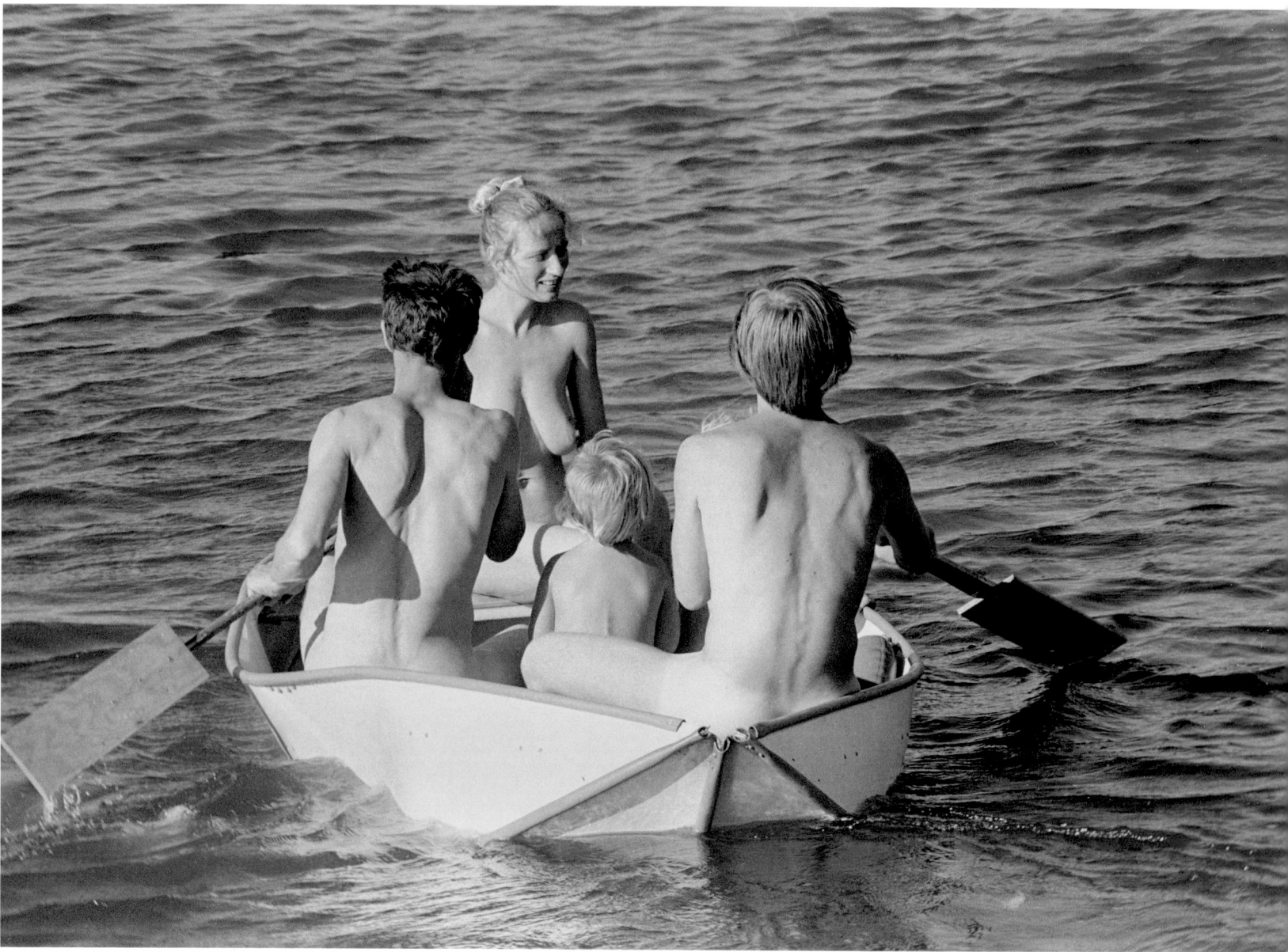

Boating on the lake.

Ole was a very recognisable figure in Christiania, usually walking around naked, often with his son Kolja, whom he treasured. Whenever he saw me, he'd come over and say, 'Mark, dear Mark'. The conversation didn't go beyond the greeting, but I appreciated his gift of uncomplicated kindliness. No one can know what is coiled inside another human being and tragically, he committed suicide some years after I took this picture. This is how I remember him, with his arms around Kolja, on a lovely summer day in the Freetown.

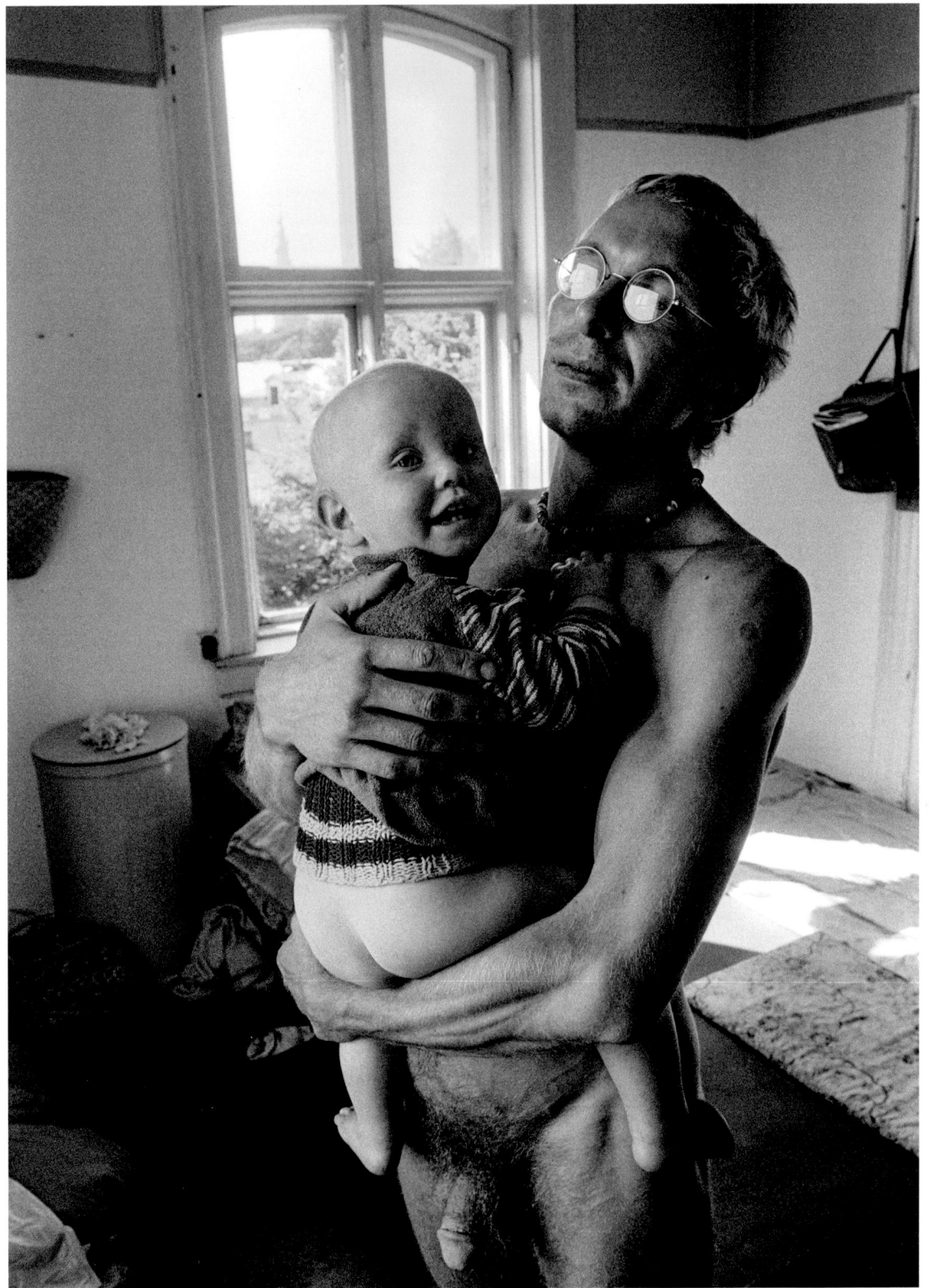

This chapter is as much about the world outside as it is about Christiania. We were, most of us, the children of parents with a very limited emotional vocabulary. The 1960s youth movement was, in part, an attempt by young people to break through to a more open way of talking about our difficulties and feelings. Christiania, which was the test bed for the 60s counterculture, offered reassuring support for people who had the courage to present themselves honestly.

Here we find people trying to work out difficulties in relationships in a community which was exploring new boundaries. Others talk about the scars inflicted by parents, teachers and wardens and their struggle to find a place in society. There is even a glimpse behind the Iron Curtain, a reminder that the Cold War was a feature of life in the 1970s.

Did the attempt to find a new emotional language help establish better relationships? Or did we walk out of one straitjacket and into another? The children who grew up in Christiania will have much to say about this.

And there is a wider question that continues to demand our attention: has society at large looked at the toll its institutions all too often inflict on its citizens? Do governments use their resources to *really* explore new approaches to the problems brought alive in these commentaries?

There are many contradictory answers, and politicians have the difficult job of figuring out the way forward. Unfortunately, they often ignore the voices of people who end up in institutions. So, this chapter is dedicated to decision makers everywhere, with a suggestion that they should listen to people at the sharp end of the debate.

# TORSTEN AND METTE

*I got to know Torsten by photographing Mette. At first, she was very reluctant but later said I could take as many photos as I liked. I taped this conversation with Torsten sitting by the window looking out at Christiania's lake, after Mette had left for Sweden.*

I first visited Christiania with another kid from my school. I used to go to an experimental school in Copenhagen and during the day I went there when I had a free period. There was a new girl from Christiania at the school that I got to know. Somehow, we got talking about the reports the teachers kept on us—if we arrived late, if we were noisy, etc. All these reports could be used against us later on. So she said, 'Well, why don't we go and burn them? Come on, let's do it—I have some matches…' I was a bit scared, but I liked being with her, talking and smoking hash… I suppose I was about fourteen or fifteen at the time.

After that, I decided to visit her in Christiania with my friend. We began to talk about things like anarchism and politics with a guy called Hvide Per, but he got tired of listening to us rambling on, so he began to masturbate his dog—that shut us up!

*What did your parents think of Christiania?*

Oh, I don't know what my parents thought—my mother and father were divorced. I lived with my father, and he always said that it was my life, and that I had to make my own decisions. Of course, he had his own opinions, and maybe he was a bit worried and didn't like me smoking hash, but he didn't interfere.

Later I lived in Fredens Ark in Christiania and met the girl I knew from school. We'd seen each other around but I finally met up with her again in the Grey Hall. We danced and it was wonderful, I fell in love with her.

One night, when I got home after seeing her, I couldn't get to sleep. So I listened to some jazz music and wrote her a letter. But she was so cool towards me that I thought that she must have met another guy. She hadn't—that's just the way she was. I gave her little presents… I was really very much in love… One day I came out here, after I had written her a letter—she kept them all—and we sat and talked, and suddenly we were holding hands, it was really very, very nice.

Later we lived together and became really wrapped up in each other. I spent all my time with her—well, I did talk to the neighbours and go to the shops once in a while—but she was very shy. When we went out, she always wanted to walk on top of the earthworks around the lake instead of along the street. When I asked her why, she said that she couldn't stand all the people looking at us.

But after a year, we began to argue, and I moved away for a while.

One day I came back to see her and we got back together again. Later we went on holiday, and that was when she got pregnant with our son.

*When did you move into Kosmiske Blomst?*

That was when all the problems started. We wanted to move because she'd had an affair. We moved around a bit within Christiania. At one stage we lived in Parthenon, but we didn't dare heat the room, because the stove used coke, and we were afraid that it would poison us. Next, we moved across the bridge to Dyssen, and then we got this room, and I started going to school again. She had the child here, in this room. I remember you visited us just after she'd given birth. But then we started arguing again. I've heard that she quarrels a lot with the guy she's living with now…

Around this time, I started to read her diaries. She tried to hide them, but I always found them. When she thought that she'd hidden them well, she would write for herself, but when she thought I was likely to find them, she wrote as if addressing me directly. I learnt that she wanted me to stay at home, and that she hated me going to school. She said that I was never home and asked if I didn't want to have some influence over our child's upbringing. We talked it over, and I explained that I didn't want to be a worker for the rest of my life just to earn money to support her and the child. She suggested that we go to Sweden to live, but I said that I wanted to finish my schooling first.

I think at first I was attracted to her because she was very beautiful, but then, as time passed, the things we did and shared together made me fall more and more in love with her. She's very reserved, while I'm a very open person, but I thought we could make it work because I loved her. At the same time, though, I also wanted to go into town, to have some fun and meet other people, but she never wanted to go. I thought that I should just do what I wanted, and see how things turned out…

At first, when we were in bed together, and we were really close, especially if we'd just made up after a row, I felt that we could really talk and she would understand everything I said, but I soon realised that she didn't understand anything, and I felt completely alone in the world. No one can understand everything you are feeling and trying to say.

I would ask her how she felt, but she was afraid, so she just withdrew even more. Then I would shout and throw things around the room. Sometimes, just to get some kind of reaction from her, I would stand in her way, until she exploded and called me a bloody fascist, or something like that. I still liked her very much, and I thought that maybe I could save her from her strange seclusion, but I started to act strangely myself. I started to hide things and act in a way that didn't reflect my true feelings.

Around the time you took that picture of Mette feeding the baby and me reading, I had a friend staying here for the winter. When he invited Mette to visit him in Sweden, she went, just so we could have a bit of a break from each other. We thought that when I finished school, I'd join her and get work, and that maybe we could buy a house there, or perhaps join a collective. At first, we wrote to each other. In one letter she'd ask me to come straight away, and in the next one she'd say that I shouldn't come, that she wanted to live alone.

When she'd been there for six months, I did go to visit her. By then she'd become very distant again. I slept with her, but sometimes I couldn't even make love to her. I got very confused. Then she told me that she was falling in love with this guy, Tom, who she'd been living with.

Well, when you've been apart for six months, something is bound to happen. Something had happened in my life too, but I didn't feel the same way as she did because I still thought that our relationship had been good.

After a time, Tom threw her out, because she didn't do anything around the house. Finally, I accepted that I had to get myself together and forget the past.

*How did you feel losing your son—that must have been very hard?*

It was harder losing Mette, because I'd only lived with my son for two or three months. Of course, we had a relationship, but he couldn't talk, and I couldn't breastfeed him. It was much harder her moving away—it affected me a lot more. After that, something changed in the way I related to women and in what I wanted from my relationships with them. That's been good, it's made me look at things in a different way.

*How was your life here in Kosmiske Blomst?*

When I first came here, the people I knew best were Soren, Sieb, Ebba, Ida and Leif (but he didn't talk much). Ida and I had a lot of fun flirting, but most of the time we'd have a bit of a banter about social issues. If our discussions got too heated and we started shouting, the rest of the them would start to complain, saying we were keeping them awake. That's how I got to know the people here. At that time, though, the only thing on my mind was my relationship with Mette, and with myself.

When I'd been here for a month, Ebba and Soren went on holiday and I was supposed to water their flowers. One evening, I'd been to do it and was just leaving, when I bumped into Tommy. He asked me what I was doing and when I told him he laughed. 'Oh, you're that lunatic—the guy who just runs around rambling on about nothing.' That was our

first contact. In the winter, we couldn't stay here. Mette was scared that the child was going to be poisoned by the fumes from the stove, so we didn't have any heating, and there was no light in our room. I got very sick, and eventually we went to live with Mette's mother. She told me that I was nothing but a hippie, eating all her food, and soon asked us to move out. Tommy and some of the others kept saying that if we didn't come back soon, they would give our room to someone else. We felt that everybody, except Leif and Ida, were our enemies.

When Mette moved out, I got to know the guys here. Tommy had had a hard time with his girlfriend, so we felt a bit like brothers, in the same boat as far as women were concerned.

None of the other guys here had girlfriends, so Tommy and I had a certain bond, and we started to do small jobs together. I became a sort of apprentice for Tommy. He taught me how to do things and we painted the bridge together. I was very impressed by the way he worked, making wood carvings and things like that. I began to focus on learning something myself from living in Christiania. The first thing I learnt was to express myself, to connect with my own emotions. Then, I tried out lots of different things, like wood carving and playing the drums with the guys here…

They only rules are practical ones—try to be independent, and don't rely too much on other people. But I couldn't manage anything on my own; I just wandered about in my own dream world. I had to eat at Tommy's place if I wanted hot food. I was very depressed, feeling that I was worthless. I was pessimistic about the future, but as time went on, I learnt one rule: you have to believe in your own ability to manage and get on in life. You start to realise that material things don't count that much; it's nice to have a good standard of living but it isn't important. What is important is that you aren't always leaning on other people.

*Did everyone take equal responsibility in the house?*

Well, Tommy was always the one who defended our place. It was always him who got rid of people we didn't like, people who stole our things—there are all kinds of strange people in Christiania. The rest of us were just too apathetic. It seemed like we didn't care, but we did, a lot; we just didn't have the courage to confront ourselves. Once, after chasing one of these crazy people out, Tommy broke down in tears, and it was then that I decided that I had to do something as well. If I felt that something was wrong, then I would have to do something about it too. That's the way we educate ourselves—by doing things with each other, not by telling each other what to do. I can't leave all the work to the others, because if I don't do my share, our experiences will be so different that we won't get on any more.

*Are you still in touch with Mette?*

Well, it's quite a long time since we've written to each other. She's pregnant by this new guy she's living with. We are still in contact, and there are no bad feelings, or anything like that—but now is a time when we have to manage our own lives . . . so, we don't write to each other. Not because we don't want to—we just don't need to.

*I met this guy soon after he came to live in Christiania. He lived in a cold, dark room in Fredens Ark.*

*How long have you lived in Christiania?*

Six months. I came straight from prison. I got three and a half years for bank robbery.

*What was it like?*

Not good. It was hard to adjust. In prison, the strongest come out on top.

*What were the fights about?*

Money problems, hash. Every Friday night I got 200g of hash, in cigarette boxes, in shoes. Everybody inside smokes. The guards don't care.

*A guy was killed in this house, wasn't he?*

Yeah, I knew him well. All the hash I sold came from him. He lived in this room where we are now. I moved in when he died. There was an argument involving some crazy guy. My friend went to cool things down and he got killed—stabbed… I just take one day at a time. I don't think about tomorrow and its problems. I could go back to prison for two years. I escaped six months ago.

*How did you get out?*

It was late at night. I cut the bars with a blade from the prison workshop—it cost me a lot—300 Kr. (£30). Altogether it cost me 2000 Kr. (£200) to get out. It took me an hour to cut through the bars, and once I got outside the cell, I had to drop seven metres to the ground. Then I had to get past the security cameras watching the compound.

*Do you still have money from the bank robbery?*

No… some of it.

*Did you get a lot of money?*

69,000 Kr. (£6900)

*How were you caught?*

It was about three weeks later, when I came back from a holiday. Someone had told the police; I don't know who. I did something and paid the price.

The cell was two and a half metres this way and four metres that way, about the same size as this room. In prison, my door was open from six o'clock in the morning to nine-thirty at night. I woke up at six, and I worked from seven till four o'clock. Then we could relax in a television room. We had a kitchen and we could play cards.

*How did you get into the bank?*

I got three and a half years because it was with a gun, although it wasn't loaded. I just ran with the money—no car, nothing. I knew the streets very well.

*What do you feel about hash? Do you wish you didn't smoke?*

I think it should be legal. I only sell it for the money, and I make good money. You see this hash? It's 30 per cent PVC. We took it to the laboratory for analysis. They said, 40 per cent cannabis, 30 per cent PVC. It's true. It's made in Holland. I have made a lot of money with it, but I never smoke it. I just sell it—it's not good for my health.

*How do you feel, selling it to other people? If it's not good for your health, it's not good for anyone.*

Yeah, you're right. If anyone asks me, I tell them it's business. It would be best to boycott it.

*How do you bring hash into Christiania?*

A girl with a child brings it in a pram.

*Do you feel you are part of a social experiment?*

I don't personally, but I think it is a social experiment. I only live here for the money. It's the best place for me.

*Do you like Christiania?*

Yes, I do.

*How long do you think you will stay?*

Till the police take me. I've been arrested twice for dealing, but they don't connect me with the robbery. I have false papers, and a false name. One day I'll go back to prison—I'll hand myself in—but first I want a holiday in Norway. Then I'll go to the police. Every day I'm looking over my shoulder. I can't do what I want—I can't live like other people. I have a wife and two children, a girl aged five and a boy of four. I phone them every day and send them money when I can. They know I'm out, but they don't know where I am. I have to do these two years in prison so I can be with them again.

*What kind of life did you lead before you went to prison?*

I worked every day. I was a cook, a top chef.

# THE TAXI-DRIVER

*After several phone calls, Mr Erik Mathisen, leader of the Uro Patrol, finally agreed to an interview. I was in the taxi on my way to see him, sorting out the tape recorder and questions, when the driver asked why I was going to the Uro Patrol headquarters. By the time I'd explained, we'd drawn up outside the office. A red car pulled out of the narrow drive. The taxi driver turned to me and said, 'I know all of those men in the car, two of them quite well, as friends. When they're not talking or thinking about Christiania, you can have a nice time with them.'*

*Well, I'd met them too. I told the taxi driver how they'd raided my room in Fredens Ark.*

*I asked him what they say about Christiania.*

They say it should be bombed. They think the people there are taking something from them. Well, I have something against Christiania myself. I think it's wrong for people just to take things. I can't go into a house and say, I want it. I have to pay, so why don't they? But I don't mind that much. I know there are good and bad people everywhere…

But there are definitely bad people there and lots of problems. I can give you an example. I have a good friend, a taxi driver, who has an eleven-year-old kid who disappeared and couldn't be found. He did everything to find his son, the police were involved, and it was even in the newspapers. Eventually they found him at a farm in Jutland, and he had been completely brainwashed. He couldn't even talk to his father. I've never seen a human being so broken. It wasn't his son who came back.

The man who did that to him was like that Guru Maharaj Ji, and he was living in Christiania. If it had been me, I would've killed him.

*I know the story of this boy and the guy who did so much harm in Christiania. He's one of the few people not allowed back into the place, so now he's making trouble somewhere else. If you close Christiania down the problems wouldn't go away.*

No, I don't think you understand. If I had the power now, I'd go down to Christiania and say, 'You have it the way you want it now, but not everybody likes it.' I would insist that they sorted the sanitation out, the baths and toilets, and the electricity too. I think the government should get involved. They should provide a medical doctor, and another one for psychological problems, drugs problems, etc. Then they should bring in some social workers to help the people who need that kind of support. If all this was done, I think something positive could come out of the place. But one thing I can tell you for sure, the Uro Patrol wouldn't go into Christiania without information.

*Are there people in Christiania, giving information to the Uro Patrol?*

Yes, for sure.

*The Uro told you this?*

No, they know what they can talk about and what they can't. I don't want to know everything about what they do. We can talk about the problems, but only up to a point.

*Have they ever asked you to work for them?*

Well, not work, but they made it clear to me that if I could come up with some information, they wouldn't be ungrateful. I once reported a man who was drunk and driving a cab. I felt very bad about it afterwards. I don't like informing against people. Also, the taxi is my work, and I can't inform against my customers. I know at least one hundred people from Christiania that I could put in jail, but why would I? They've never done anything wrong to me. I never have problems with these people, and they pay me what they owe for their fares.

*Do the Uro guys see anything good about Christiania?*

No, why should they? Christiania is just a problem to them. They see people drinking too much, and when people drink, they don't know what they're doing. I've driven a lot of people to clinics and hospitals. Sometimes you see a young guy, maybe just fifteen years old, but completely wasted. I know one in particular. He buys hash there every night. The thought that somebody is making money out of him makes me really angry. The Uro Patrol should go after the dealers, not the users. Dealers are really dangerous, and I don't care if they hang them or shoot them. I couldn't care less. Obviously, everybody has to make money, but not by harming other people. That's the sort of man I want the Uro Patrol to get.

*The Christianites want to cooperate with the police over narcotics, but the Uro Patrol won't respond.*

Okay, the police will never get anywhere if they don't work with the people, so I don't understand that. I don't want trouble with the police, because I'd like to know that they would come and help me if I were in trouble. A lot of taxi drivers have big problems. They get beaten up, their money is taken and sometimes even their cars are stolen. But not by people from Christiania. They would never do that.

*We said goodbye and I went to meet Mr Mathisen, but he refused to talk. He seemed rather to have enjoyed the inconvenience of my wasted journey…*

*He used to come up to me and say, 'What are you actually doing, Mark, I mean, what are you really doing with all those photographs you take?' Then he'd roar with laughter and ride off on his stolen bike. Once he came up to me when I was on my bike and I cycled off with him and explained. But here is his story.*

When I was twelve, I was given a choice—do you want to go to school or do you want to go to work? I chose work. I left home every morning at seven o'clock and came back at midnight. In the end I lived at work—home was just so fucked up. Finally, I left and went to England and worked at a stables. It was really nice—most of the work was exercising the horses. When you fell off, you had to get up immediately and run after the horse, because it was worth more than you were. But then I got ringworm. I was locked up, or rather I was isolated, for three months. All my clothes were taken and burnt. When I got better, they gave me £50—they said it was my fault that I got infected. So that's how I worked—for the very rich, for very little money, and that's how they get rich. At the stable I was getting £1.30 a week. I used to con the rest of my money playing cards with the other guys every Friday night.

By the time I was fifteen or sixteen and back in Ireland I was looking for a bit more than that. Eventually I was caught stealing and was taken before the judge, a Mrs Kennedy, who said, 'This boy's uncontrollable, he'll have to go away for two years.' They stuck me in the reformatory. All you had to do—all you could do—was walk around a big square all day long. All you got to talk about with the other people there was: How much did you rip off? How much did you con? How much did you steal? If you did *anything* wrong, you got caned.

I broke out of there after six weeks. There was a big fucking wall the height of this building, but I got over it with another guy and we ran all the way to Dublin.

We got over by putting railway sleepers two metres long against it and crawling up with our feet pressed against them. When we got to the top, we had to jump down: there was such a shock from the knees up. We ran along a canal; everybody who saw us knew where we were from, so the only thing to do was to get on to the railway tracks. I knew the railway, so I knew which way to go. I knocked on the door at home, and they said, 'You don't live here any more'. So I ended up sleeping in a factory where they made plastic bags to put fertiliser in. The next day I was caught—two pigs came for me. They said, you've had a nice time, lad, but you're going back now…

*Is it very hard in prison?*

No, no, it's as easy as you make it. I used to hang around in borstal with a guy I was doing two years with. We were so fucking anti-authority—we knew we were, we used to play tricks on the prison staff. I spent most of the time in solitary confinement. It was the best school of meditation I've been to. Because all I could do was meditate. I couldn't even pick up the Bible, because I couldn't read. You had to get up at six o'clock in the morning and take the big wooden bed that you'd slept on out of your cell into another room and wait for breakfast—you got porridge, two slices of bread and a piece of butter. Then a prison warden came along, and it was up to him to play his own individual games with you. You had to do physical exercise, press-ups or whatever he decided.

*How do you think the wardens saw you?*

I don't think they saw anything. I think they just saw me as part of their routine. They just play their games with you. But the con plays his own tricks too, he doesn't let it get to him. I didn't let it get to me. I played Buddha. There was nothing else for me to do.

When I finally got out, after I'd done my time, my old man gave me £5 for the boat, and I went to England. I left Ireland because the pigs were getting to haunt me every day of the week, and they were haunting my old man. He told me to get out, because I was a disgrace to the family. I had no option but to leave, so I got up and got out. I saw an advertisement in a Sunday paper for workers at an abattoir in Denmark, so I did six months there. I came to Copenhagen with 4000 Kr. (£400). While I was at the abattoir, someone told me about Christiania, and I ended up in Woodstock. I was looking for a place to sleep, that was the most important thing at that point. And, of course, I was hassled. Jørgen came along; he wanted me to give him his elephants back! I didn't know what the fuck to do. I didn't know whether to knock him out, or to get out. But I stayed.

The only job I do here is pushing. I don't work much, apart from working for Christiania. I don't mean that I work in the physical sense but by being here I am working for Christiania.

Shall I tell you about my passport? It will really surprise you. I was supposed to have lost it, right, and I went to the Irish embassy to get another one. They contacted Ireland and told me when I went to collect it that they couldn't issue one. They gave me a three-day passport to leave the country, so I went back home and applied for a full passport in Dublin. I was taken into a small office and the guy turned to me and said, 'I'm sorry we can't issue you with a passport—you have to go to the Ministry of Foreign Affairs.' When I went there, I was literally told to get out.

A lawyer took up my case, but he couldn't get anywhere with it. So, I had to leave the country with a forged passport and right now I'm subject to five years for forgery. They gave me no option—what the fucking hell are you supposed to do?

*I had tried to talk with Anna lots of times, but she was very reserved and we could not get beyond her shyness and my awkwardness. But one day we met and just talked. I had no idea about her background and this astonishing glimpse behind the Iron Curtain took me completely by surprise. She was living in a beautiful room in Christiania with three cats, which you had to watch very carefully—it was terribly cold outside and of course the cats had no intention of going out to piss if they could help it. For reasons that will become evident, references to Anna's country of origin have been omitted.*

I've had a really strange life. My mother kept me away from my father—she told me he'd tried to kill me as a baby. I only saw him a few times but just before I left my country, we became neighbours.

I decided to leave when I was at university. Deciding to travel abroad isn't the same as it is for you. Where I come from you have to escape, like a criminal getting out of prison.

When I left the country, my father came to the station. Suddenly tears rolled down his cheeks and I knew he was seeing me for the first time as his daughter. And I could see this man for the first time as my father. I cried too. I cried all night, knowing that I would never see him again.

I studied psychology for five years and after my degree I won a scholarship to study philosophy. I knew when I started the course that I would leave the country. I'd always wanted to travel, but I didn't have any money and besides, I couldn't get a passport. It was a really long-term plan! Eventually I was given papers to travel abroad for one month. They wouldn't give my boyfriend permission, but I went anyway because I wanted to make contacts abroad so we would have somewhere to go if we got the chance to leave together.

I travelled to Norway to visit people I'd met in my country, and they gave me an address to visit. It was Christiania. My first impressions were bad! I was shocked; it was so different from my country. When I returned home, my friends were tremendously impressed. Friends kept coming round, just to hear about Christiania.

Gradually we made preparations to leave for good—we had to bribe officials to get passports. It was very difficult. First, we needed to get money. The best thing to buy and sell there is a flat, and to get a flat you have to get married. However, it's easier to get a passport when you're divorced, so we got married and got a flat then got divorced and sold the flat. With the money we'd raised we bought our passports. It cost maybe $500 plus vodka just for the man who knew the officials. That really is a lot of money in my country.

It's very difficult to make contact with the police to get permission to go abroad. You have to do it through one of their family members—for example a cousin or father-in-law. We met one guy with relations in the police, a lucky break, and we started to drink with him and his friends—awful people, awful. It took more than six months to make friends with him. It was only then that we started to talk about how we wanted to go on holiday to Greece for a fortnight. He introduced us to his uncle, who was worse. Both of them drank a lot, so before every meeting we had to drink some oil to line our stomachs so as not to get drunk. If we'd got drunk, we might have lost everything. We had to keep our heads clear and carefully watch what they were doing—we had to play-act all the time.

When they were drunk, they said to us, 'We'll give you a passport, but we'll also give you the address of a guy who lives in France. You must kill him for us.' And they meant it. It sounds ludicrous now, but we had to play along with it.

But finally, we contacted the right person, a retired but very important policeman, who gave a recommendation to somebody in police headquarters. First, we had to pay the old guy, who then signed a document for the police, guaranteeing our return.

A double life and a double morality are normal in my country. People have two faces, one for family and friends, and one for neighbours and work…

*Did your parents get into trouble because you did not return?*

My mother, I don't know—I've had no contact with her. But my father wrote to me very cautiously—you can't write in a normal way because they censor letters. He told me they'd demoted him, so he has less money than before. I felt really bad when I read that…

Now the authorities want to use me! When I went to the embassy to renew my passport, they said, 'You are highly educated, you can tell us what's going on in Denmark and Copenhagen.' I refused and ran out of the building. So now they won't renew my passport, and the Danish police won't renew my visa without a valid passport, so I don't know what to do…

We had originally planned to go to Holland when we left, but somehow we ended up in Denmark, so we decided to visit a girl I'd met on my first trip who lives in Christiania. She invited me to stay here, saying there were a lot of nice people who would help me, and after a week I met a guy who offered to marry me so I could get Danish citizenship. I didn't leave my country for money; I just wanted to be free to live in my own way. In Christiania you can do that.

Now I work in the bakery and for the first time in my life I'm working with my hands. To begin with, it didn't feel right, because all my life I've worked with my brain, but now I'm fine with it. It's no good if you can only use your hands to hold a pen or open a book.

*That's almost like the Chinese Communist idea that the intellectual should spend time on the land.*

Yes, I used to think that the system I'd encountered in my country was the only form of communism, but now I've found real communism here. It's a classless society. There are differences between people, of course—but there aren't real classes like in normal society.

But the first few months in Christiania, trying to get to know people, were very difficult. The first step is to get work. If you're working in Christiania, you become a Christianite.

*What's your daily routine?*

When I wake up, I have to cut wood. It takes a lot of time to collect it, dry it and cut it ready for burning. Today it took me around four hours, but the wood will only last two days because it's so cold.

*Is this the best life for you?*

Yes… well, maybe it isn't the best, but it's better than my own country and I'm satisfied with what I have.

When we first came to Christiania, we lived in Fakirskolen: eight people living in one big room—strange people, not a collective, nothing like that. It was really hard, what with Isabella shooting her gun in the night. She had a real gun, and she would shoot it at the ceiling and the walls.

*How did you, a psychologist, feel living in a community where crazy people aren't separated and locked up, but are an important part of the community?*

I'd always had good experiences when I worked in psychiatric hospitals. I never treated the patients as crazy, I just treated them as people. I mean, if people are born without brains, that's different, but if people are born normal, and after some experience in their life they start to think in another way, that's no reason to say they're crazy. They're just different. They're able to live by themselves—as Isabella, Karl and Jørgen do in Christiania. They need help, but you can't always be there for them. They have to be responsible for themselves.

Isabella, for instance, was in hospital for three years when she lived in Copenhagen. She had electric shock treatment and other things. But since she's been here she's stopped drinking, and she isn't aggressive any more—she doesn't use knives. I think Christiania has helped her a lot.

# TWO PUSHERS

*These two guys lived down the corridor from me when I lived in Fredens Ark. We got off to a bad start. The wiring in that building was in a terrible state of repair and in winter people plugged electric fires into the lighting circuit so the cables overheated. It's just luck that there haven't been any serious fires.*

*My electric supply came from the light socket in the toilet. I only used it to recharge the batteries of my flash gun and for a lamp—but someone else tapped my cable and wired a fire into it. The wire got hot and started to burn. The 'First Pusher' ripped the cable down. When I came back, I told the guy with the fire to find his own bloody socket and I rewired my line. Next day the 'First Pusher' ripped it down again. I explained that it was now safe, but he said he would rip it down every time I put it up. He didn't want to become 'roast beef', he said and slammed his door shut.*

*English diplomacy and Danish tolerance saved the day, but that was not the only problem between us. He was learning to play the electric guitar, which was fine but not at three o'clock in the morning. I put my tape recorder just outside the door, recorded his efforts, and waited until he was asleep. Then I played it back at full volume. After that we became friends. My electric supply was left alone, and we came to an amicable arrangement about the guitar practice.*

*If Christiania closes, what will you do?*

2nd Pusher: Well, I plan to study next year . . .

1st Pusher: [laughing quietly] He'll be a dealer.

2nd Pusher: Yeah, hash is a problem for me. It's a problem when I don't get it. You could say I'm addicted to it. There are good and bad things about it.

1st Pusher: Pushers have always got a lot of stuff, and when you get a lot of it, you smoke a lot of it—too much. I think pushers smoke more than the people who grow it, and if you really smoke a lot, then you're as hooked as if you smoked fifty cigarettes a day.

Some people who smoke hash say, 'Oh, hash is beautiful, and it isn't dangerous' and things like that. That's a lie! Hash is dangerous and hash is very bad for your health. I don't want young people to smoke it. I think it's more dangerous than alcohol. We didn't know that when we started to smoke, but we do now.

*Well, how do you feel selling what you regard as a dangerous drug?*

1st Pusher: I think that I'm a bastard, and I think that the only way to survive is to be a bastard—it's survival of the fittest.

2nd Pusher: I think it's okay to sell the stuff you use yourself. I like to smoke hash. I really like it.

1st Pusher: Yeah, yeah, he really likes it! [laughter]

2nd Pusher: Yeah, I want to smoke hash for the rest of my life, if I can afford it.

*Don't you feel you are just dreaming your life away? Do you think you will ever stop smoking dope?*

1st Pusher: I do try sometimes, and I would really like to stop. Not totally, but to just smoke once or twice a week. I think that a lot of people want that, but very few of them actually say so.

2nd Pusher: Yeah, I used to be the same, but I've given up that line of thinking.

*Do you think hash should be legalised?*

2nd Pusher: Yes, it should be.

1st Pusher: No, it shouldn't be legalised. We've already got alcohol problems—then we'd have hash-damaged people like us as well, who can't work. What can we do? We can't survive in the outside world. Young people shouldn't smoke hash. I started when I was fourteen or fifteen and I shouldn't have. I can see that today, but I did, and if I see young people on Pusher Street, [the area where most of the dealers operate] I won't sell to them. Okay, so they get it from someone else, but I won't touch their money. It's dirty money.

2nd Pusher: In ten years it won't be so exciting, because it will be legal.

*Have you been arrested by the police?*

1st Pusher: Yeah, lots of times. When I was fifteen or sixteen, I stole a car, but the first time I was arrested I was visiting my girlfriend. I used to live in a children's home, but I was thrown out because they felt I was old enough to find my own place. I did find a place, but my girlfriend still lived there. I used to visit her but the people in charge didn't allow us to smoke or drink and I couldn't stay there. But I did anyway, so they would come into her room sometimes, even when we were fucking, and tell me to go away. I was sixteen or seventeen! When I refused to go, they called the police and said I couldn't visit any more, but I still used to go and sleep there, and whenever I thought they'd called the police, I would run away. I was caught twenty or thirty times, and then my girlfriend was thrown out too, so we started living together. After that, I was arrested for smashing shop windows and now I am picked up for selling hash.

At first, the police were really kind. They knew it was because I wanted to see my girlfriend. But when we started to smash windows and steal cars, they weren't so kind, although even then they weren't too hard on us. The first time I ever saw police violence was when we demonstrated against the World Bank. The second time was in this room. I heard them coming and yelled 'Uro Patrol' to warn some people who had a lot of hash, and then ran to your room to make the police think I was living there. They broke my arm and held me so I couldn't breathe, and then they hit me hard to make me talk but I held out. They knew the stuff was here, but they couldn't find it.

You know, every flat in Fredens Ark has somewhere to hide hash, and the police could find it if they looked, but they don't have the time. They don't like to stay here long because they're afraid of violence breaking out and being outnumbered. So it's fast. I can tell you—I hope you don't tell the police: under the doorstep, which you can remove, there's a hole. The police stand on the step and look everywhere, but they never find it. There are lots of other places. There's an old stove where you can put it, for instance, and the police never like to go through the rubbish bin. There's a lot you can do!

*Have you ever been in prison?*

1st Pusher: Yes, it was hard. You don't have anyone to talk to, and you don't know how long you'll be there.

2nd Pusher: Yeah, I was in prison for a month, when I was eighteen. It was really tough, the worst thing I've ever experienced, and I don't ever want to be inside again. It took me six months to get back to normal when I came out.

1st Pusher: Yeah, I couldn't remember what you did when you got on a bus… You're completely lost when you come out. You don't talk to anyone, or do anything in prison, just count the days until you can get out. Then when you're out, wow, a lot of things happen suddenly…

2nd Pusher: When you meet people you know, you have no confidence…

1st Pusher: But I do remember some of the cops in jail were really nice. Some were bastards, of course, but for the last twenty days when I wasn't in solitary, I could smoke hash. They didn't mind.

*How did hash get into prison?*

1st Pusher: Oh, some prisoners are allowed out at weekends, and they put it up their arse. Or if your girlfriend visits you, she just gives you the hash when she kisses you.

2nd Pusher: I know a guy who could take 160 grams of hash up his arse!

*There's a flat opposite Christiania that the police use to photograph all the dealers, isn't there?*

1st Pusher: Yeah. I know one of the guys—he busted me once down on Pusher Street, and I said, 'Don't grab me like that, I do karate, I could kill you.' That's what I told him, ha, but he said I could take it easy, because he was a black belt. He went to the same teacher as me, the World Master; he's been going for four years, and I've only been going for two. Later on, we went to the police station to write up the report. That took about five minutes, and then we spent an hour talking about karate. Anyway, I asked him about the photos, and he said they didn't have the right equipment, because the lens they needed was too expensive. But we know they watch with a telescope, because we can see them. They radio to the other cops—I think that's how they're able to arrest the pushers so easily. It would be a good picture for you, wouldn't it? But mostly they arrest foreign pushers, because they have more power over them. They aren't so hard on the Christiania pushers, because this is a social experiment. If you live here, you are part of the experiment.

*Do you pay the Christiania rent and tax?*

1st Pusher: No. If you paid, somebody might think you were afraid and had to prove that you live here, so that's not the way. You just say, 'I live here'; then you live here. You can do whatever you like with the building you're in. You can make a noise at four o'clock in the morning if you want, and only the tough guys will have the balls to come and complain.

It's the tough who survive. Anyone can come into your room and say, 'Get out, I'm stronger than you, give me your room.' It's survival of the fittest—that's very clear in Christiania.

*Why do you think there is such a gap between the pushers and the rest of Christiania?*

1st Pusher: There are lots of reasons. Maybe the people who aren't pushing haven't got so much money. Or maybe they're really idealistic, and the pushers aren't.

2nd Pusher: The idealistic people have found a way to live. The pushers are searching for a way to live. The pushers aren't really happy—they're only interested in material things.

1st Pusher: Oh no, no, no. I think it's wrong to say pushers only want money. A lot of them are like me. Maybe it's because we're still young, so feel we have to make an impression. Everybody my age or younger has a lot of problems, you know. Okay, if I get the material things, then I've got half of what I need, but I think pushers want the other half too, the idealistic things. But because we're so young, we're a bit reckless, so we say, 'To hell with it!' We make a lot of money from hash.

*One of the ideals of the people you call 'activists' is living together without comparing themselves with each other. In your world, judging yourself against the people around you sounds very important.*

1st Pusher: And a lot of idealists say, 'It doesn't matter how you look', and they mean it kindly, but it does make a lot of difference. People are the same, whatever they say. There's some difference, but basically people are all the same—you learn that here. The beautiful man and the beautiful woman are together, and the ugly man and the ugly woman are together. It's true for the activists, it's true for the pushers, and it's true in the outside world. It would be good if we could stop wars, and it's great that we're not running around killing each other, but really, it's still survival of the fittest, and, you know, if every little weak man survived, humankind would be only little weak men, and then it would die out. It's logical that we must kill some of the weakest.

*Well, it's only logical because logic doesn't take into account humanitarian values.*

1st Pusher: It's not idealistic, but it's the only way. I'd be very sorry for the men who wouldn't survive, and I'm sure that I'd be one of them—I'm one of the weakest. The activists say they'll create a world where the weak will be able to live, and everybody will be your brother. Christiania is that place, and it doesn't work. There are too many weak people here.

*Does it matter to you that people outside think of you as social losers, the weak ones, the guys who can't make a living, except by selling hash, who just sit around and smoke all day long— people who end up doing nothing with your lives?*

1st Pusher: We are at the bottom of the social pyramid. When you're a dealer, you have to be a bastard to survive. It's a luxury to be a good man, to be an idealist.

For the last five years, I've been employed by a private firm on a government contract to catch rats here. Actually, there's no great rat problem—there are too many dogs and cats for that.

Before I came here, everyone told me what an awful place it was, so at first, I felt quite negative about it. But then I got to know a few people and I realised that what I'd been told wasn't true. It was a way of living that I'd never experienced before.

Before I knew what Christiania was really like, I met a young man who'd recently graduated, a very intelligent guy. He'd been working at a home for kids with learning disabilities, and a couple of them had grown really fond of him. He was reprimanded for this, as he was not supposed to get involved with the children, or show them any favour, even if he felt he could help them in some way. He left his job, deeply depressed and asked me whether I thought he should move into Christiania. I advised him against it, because at the time I was still an opponent of the Freetown. I bitterly regret that now, because this man went on to hang himself. Now I've come to believe that Christiania is capable of solving some of the problems connected with that lack of flexibility in ordinary conformist society.

I'd been told that Christianites were only a bunch of antisocial individuals, sponging off society without wanting to contribute anything in return. I found this to be untrue. The social structure is different here—humanity is at the heart of it, not material status symbols as in wider society.

My friends still have a negative attitude towards Christiania. They're influenced by what they read in the newspapers, which only report the negative aspects of life here and nothing about the positive things going on.

There's a humane environment here, a positive climate where people can thrive, and I feel that if I was depressed about things, I could come here and find new spirit and energy.

I'm grateful to many of the people I've met here—people like Leonard. We met one winter's day many years ago and got talking. I remembered that I'd read about him in the newspapers. I realised that this was the Leonard who'd got involved with helping drug addicts. I told him that I was interested in the work he was doing and would like to support him. I think I gave him 100 Kr. (£10). He said, 'Well, how about that? I'm a person of faith, I believe in our Good Lord. I didn't have a single penny, and now God sends you—that's the way it always goes.' Sometime later, Leonard told me that he needed a car for his work, and I told him that I would try to arrange it. Originally, I thought of approaching people who could afford to give Leonard a car, but then I thought, I have a car, so why not let Leonard have it? I could then buy a small van, which would

suit me fine. He's had it for about two years now, and I think it's been useful for his work.

I've been called by the police a few times, asking me whether I was aware that my car was parked in Christiania. And when I tell them that I'm well aware of it, and that it's with Leonard by agreement, they are extremely surprised. I've since contacted the police, suggesting they form a contact group for better cooperation, but I got nowhere—most of the police are very unsympathetic.

I like Christiania very much indeed, and I'll be sorry if we lose it. But I'm too old—I'm seventy—to move in. However, if I were a young man…

Christiania is just one big problem for me. Last week I had 800 Kr. stolen. Then two days ago a junkie came to me and said, 'Betty, please help me, I'm sick—I need some money for a fix.' So I offered to help. I'd received my benefits that day and I had some money I made on the Street selling hash. I gave him the money and went to sleep in my room, but when I woke up, he'd taken the rest of the money and my hash. I'm no angel but the way some people, especially junkies, behave… They just live for themselves. I should know by now—I've lived in this world so long… I don't see the good things in people any more, just the bad things.

*Four months later Betty died. She had been fixing for a long time. Many people in Christiania tried to help her give up junk but somehow the cures never worked. In fact, she never stopped seeing 'the good things in people' and the junkies she was with never stopped taking advantage of her.*

*Ray is the archetypal hippie and looks it. I think he was originally from London, but he's been on the road a long time and his origins have worn away. We talked sitting on the platform above his workshop, surrounded by people. I never saw him on his own.*

At first, I couldn't find any privacy in Christiania—people always coming and going and things happening day and night—but you get to like it. Now if nobody's around I go and look for someone to talk to. I share my bedroom with twelve people, not always the same twelve, and I really like it. You can still have your privacy, but you're never lonely.

For me, what's so beautiful here is that whatever you do, you do it in a group. You learn to live with other people, and you rely on them and they rely on you. It's not a duty and it's not forced… it's all about respect for your fellow human beings, a responsibility that comes from within, not from outside. There's no authority telling you what to do, it's just something that develops between a group of people.

You see, if you work collectively, it's much easier. If you feel tired you just doze off, but if you were in a normal job you'd have to carry on even if your work suffered…

I first came to Christiania because somebody told me that you could get food and somewhere to sleep here. Then I realised it was a good place to meet people and spend time with them. Eventually the people who lived and worked together formed a sort of family. We broke up for a while, but then we all came back together again.

Christiania is made up of these 'families'—people in them even relate to each other as if one was a grandfather and one a grandchild or whatever. In society, generally, the family model is breaking down, but I think everyone still has a yearning to be part of a family. I was alone for about nine years—always travelling on my own—and, I think, although I didn't realise then, I was really looking for this family all the time.

# FACES

I converted my truck into a photo booth and invited people to sit for me. I would pick them up from their homes on my Long John, a delivery bike with a large platform between the handlebars and the front wheel, and cycle them to the 'studio'. A large dog adopted me. He used to run alongside us licking our faces, radiating happiness. These cycle rides were something of an exercise in trust and a good beginning to the photo session.

Black Hannah

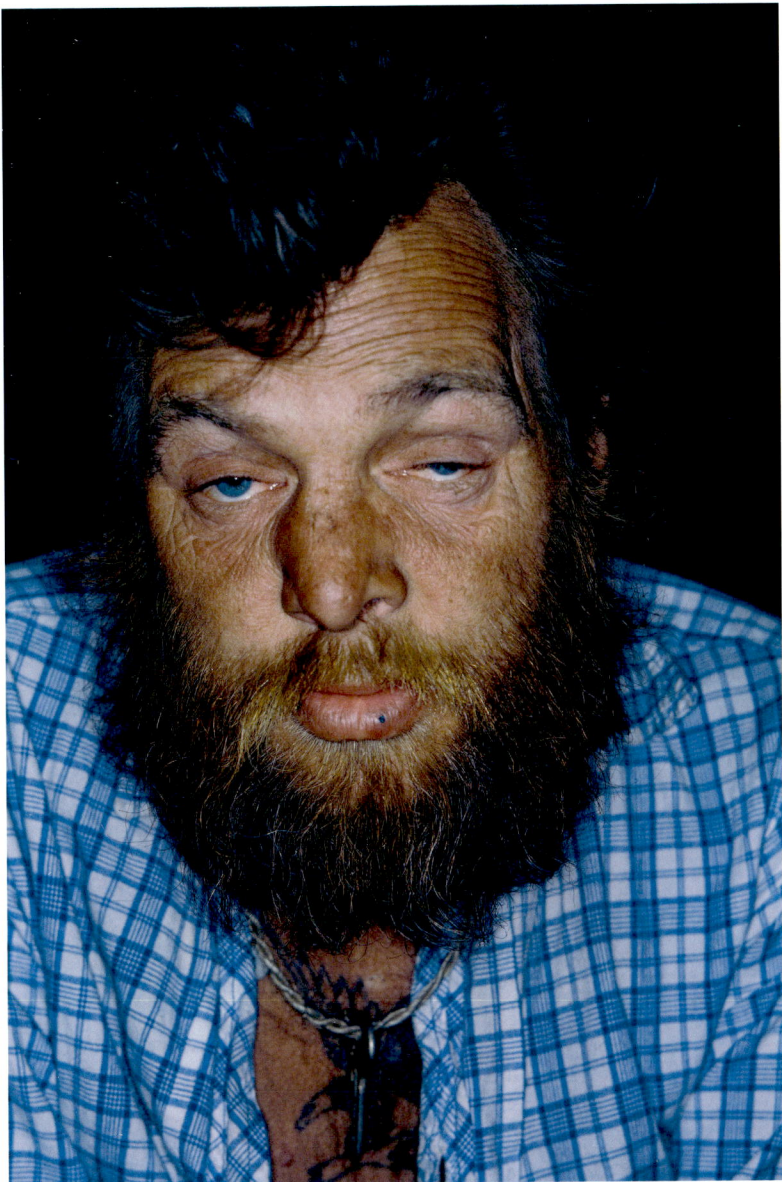

Danny

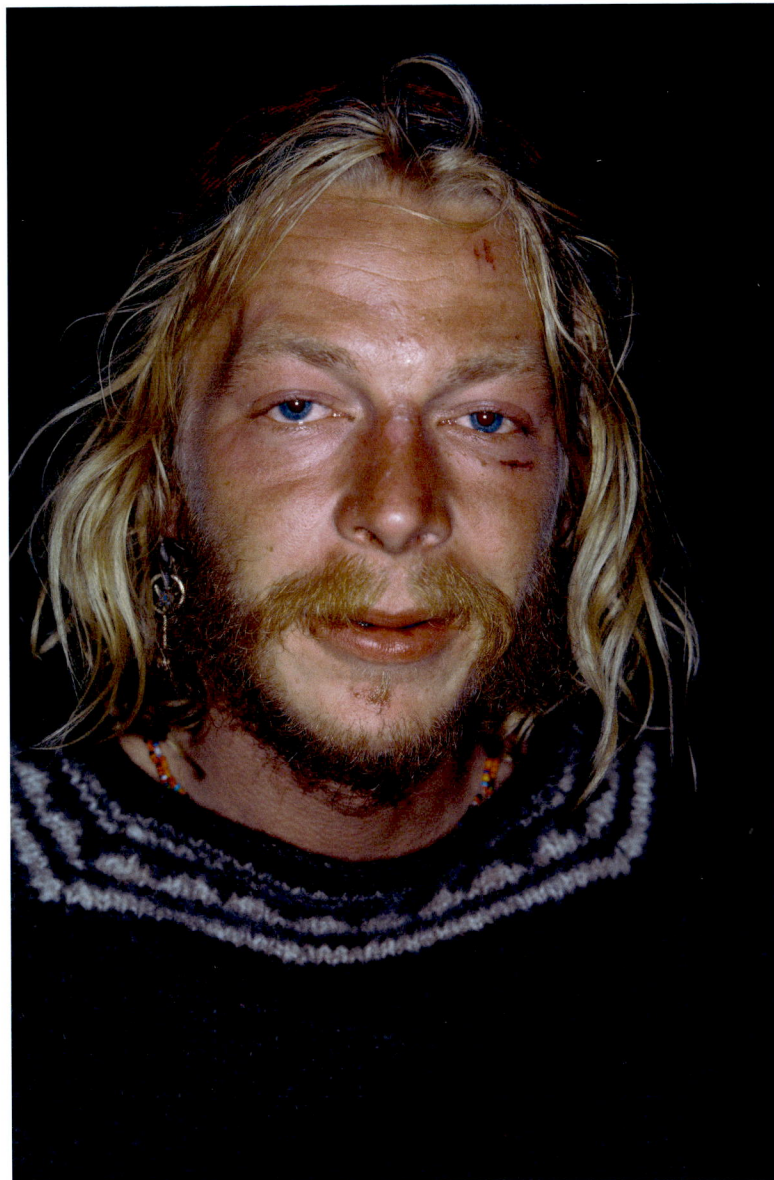

Ole

Leonard

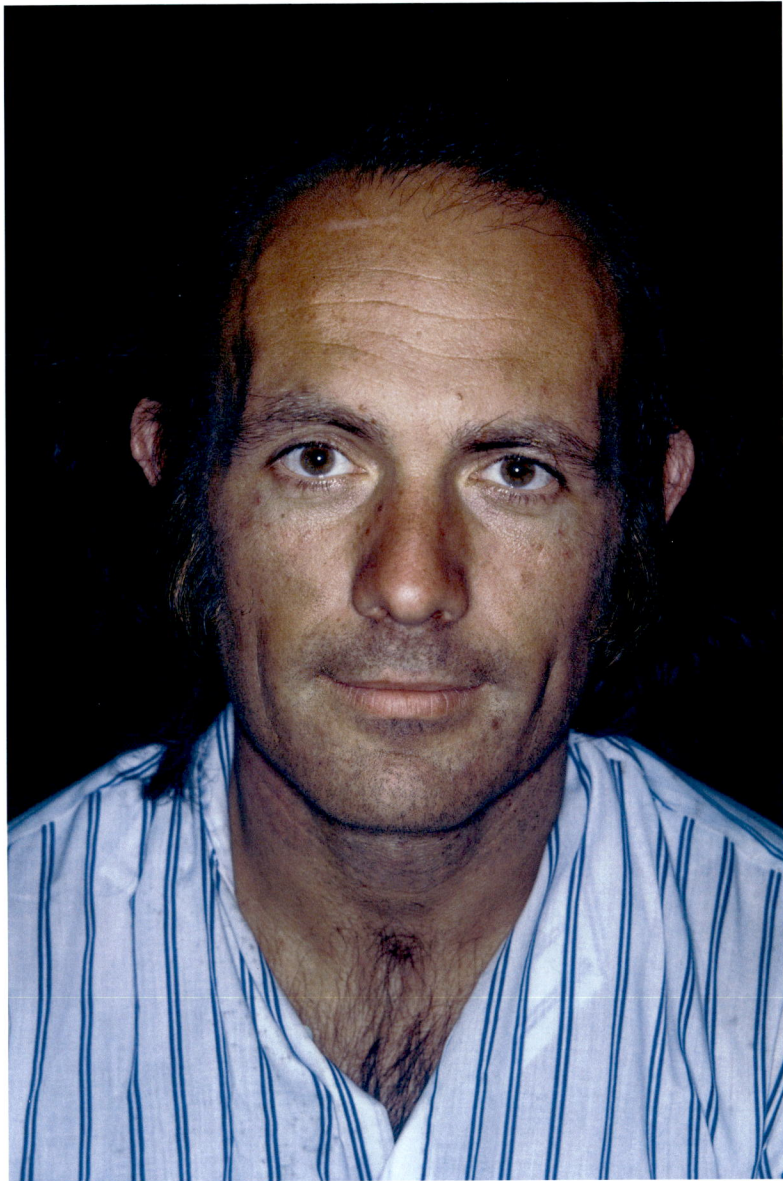

Bill

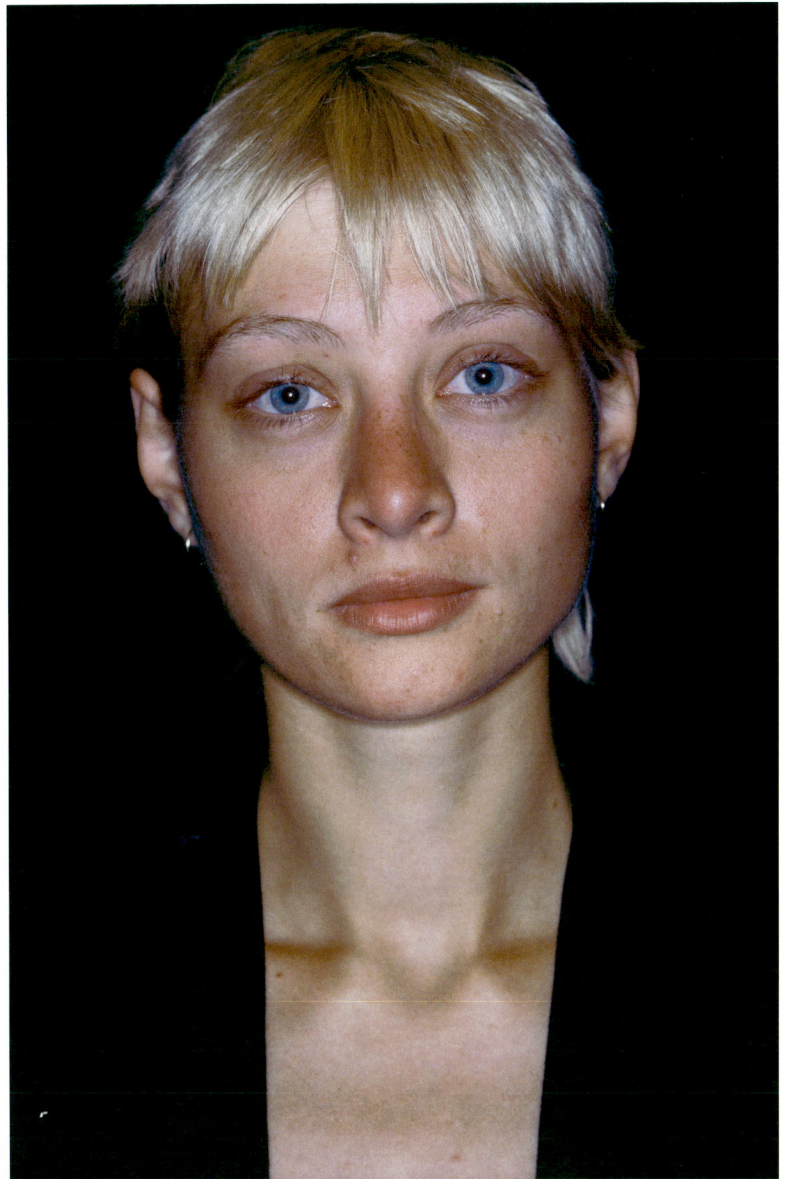

Elsie

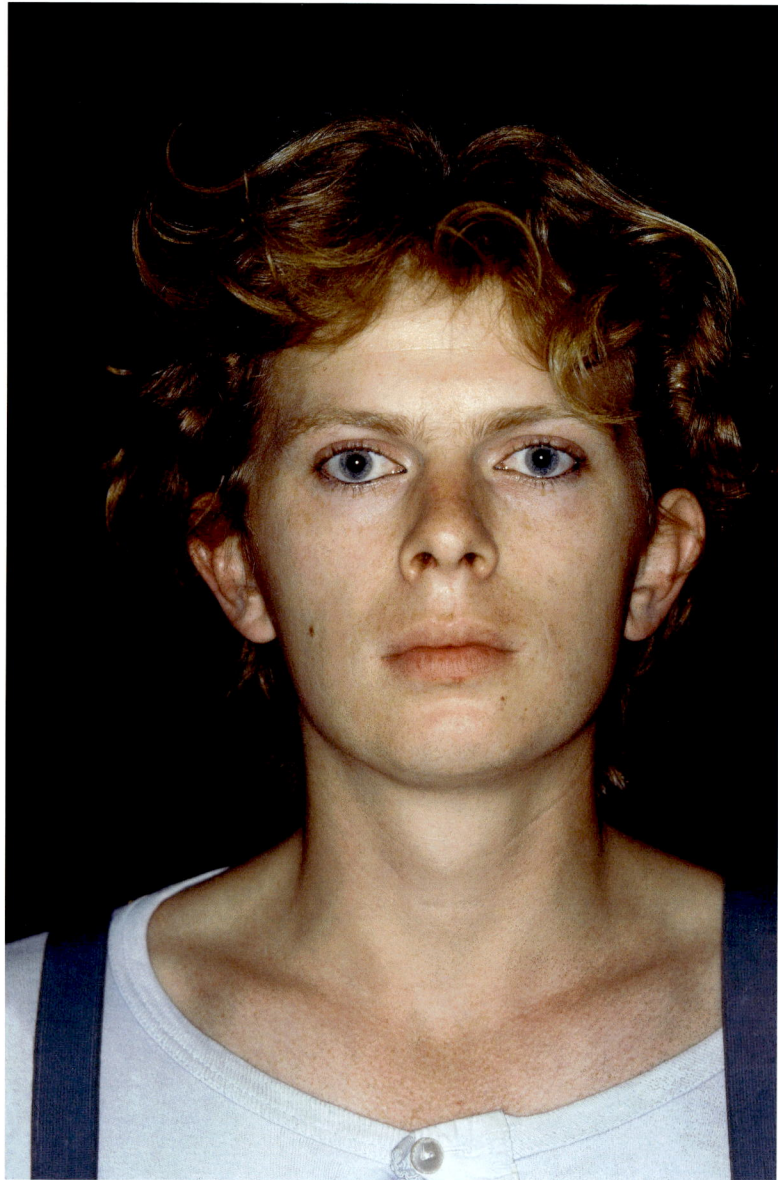

Dinesen

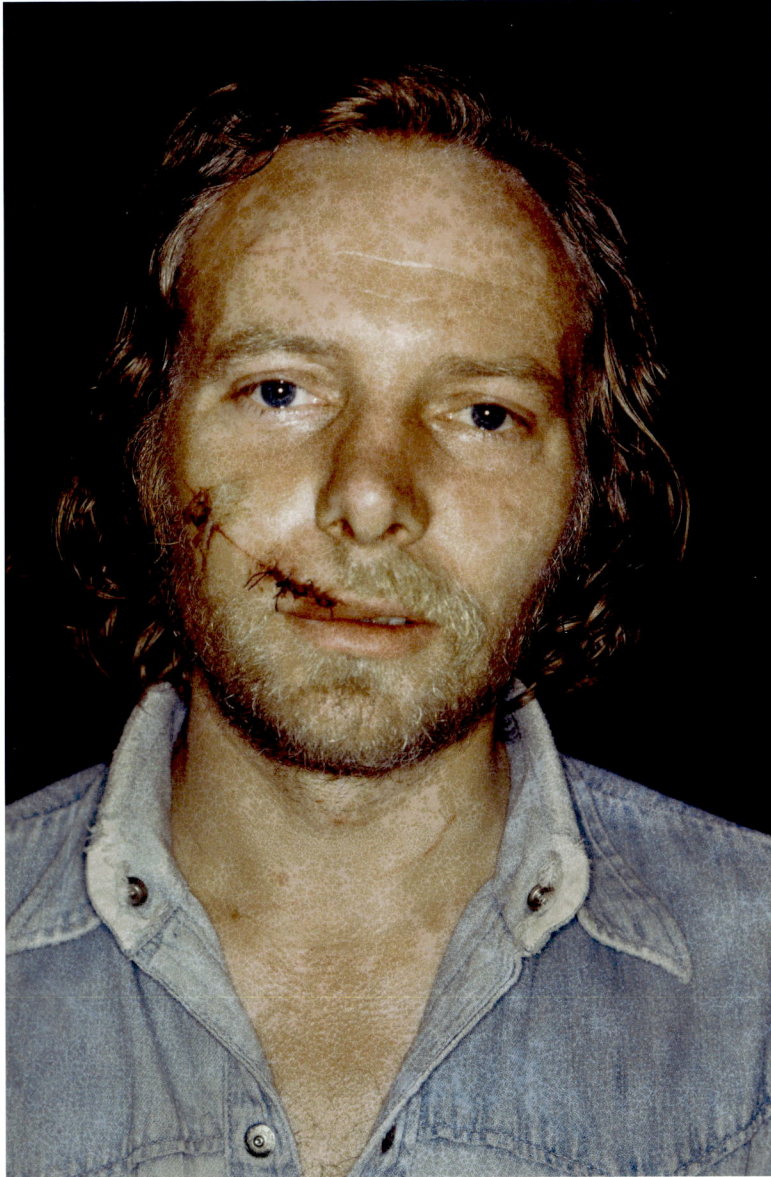

Mick

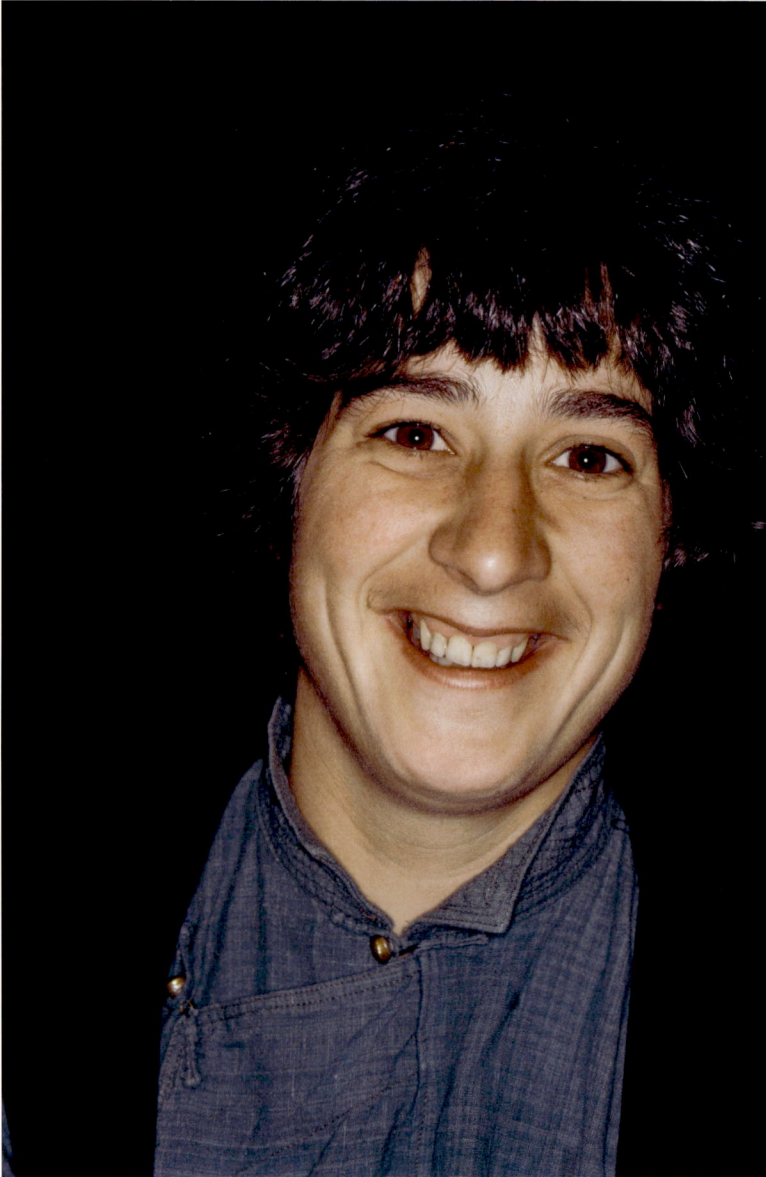

Donarta

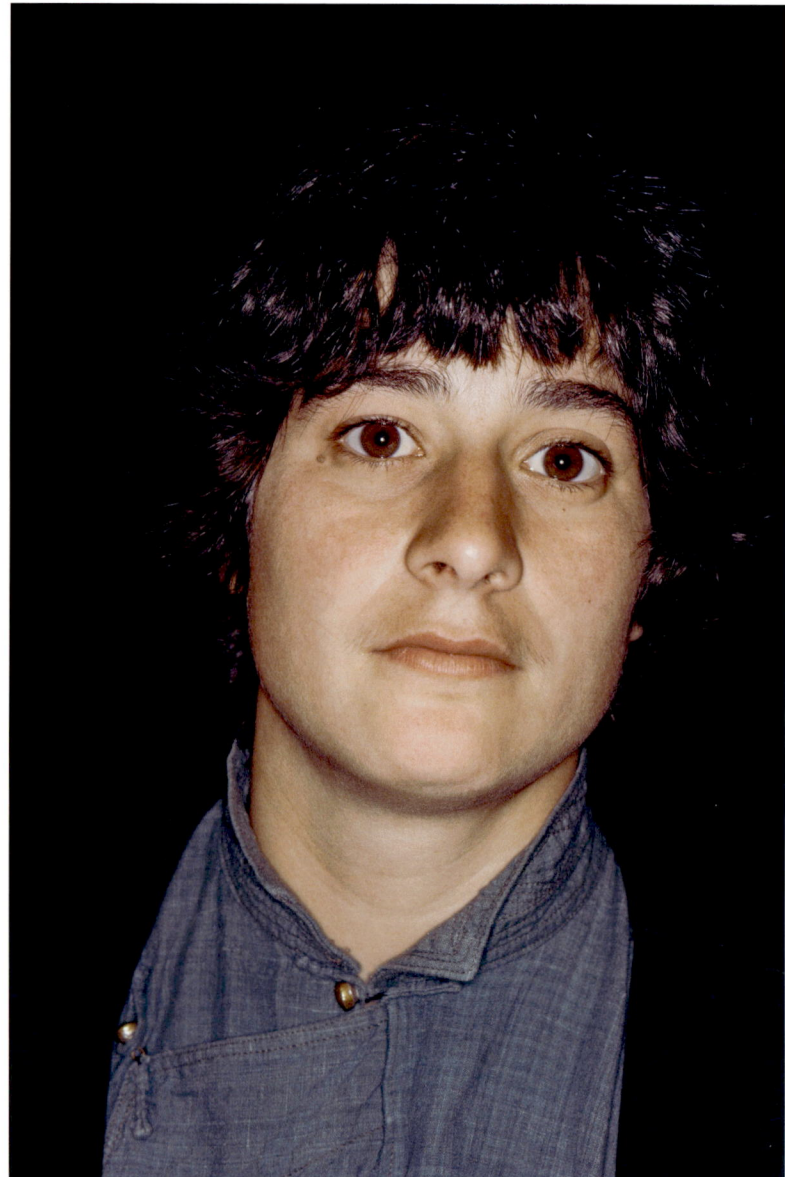

Donarta

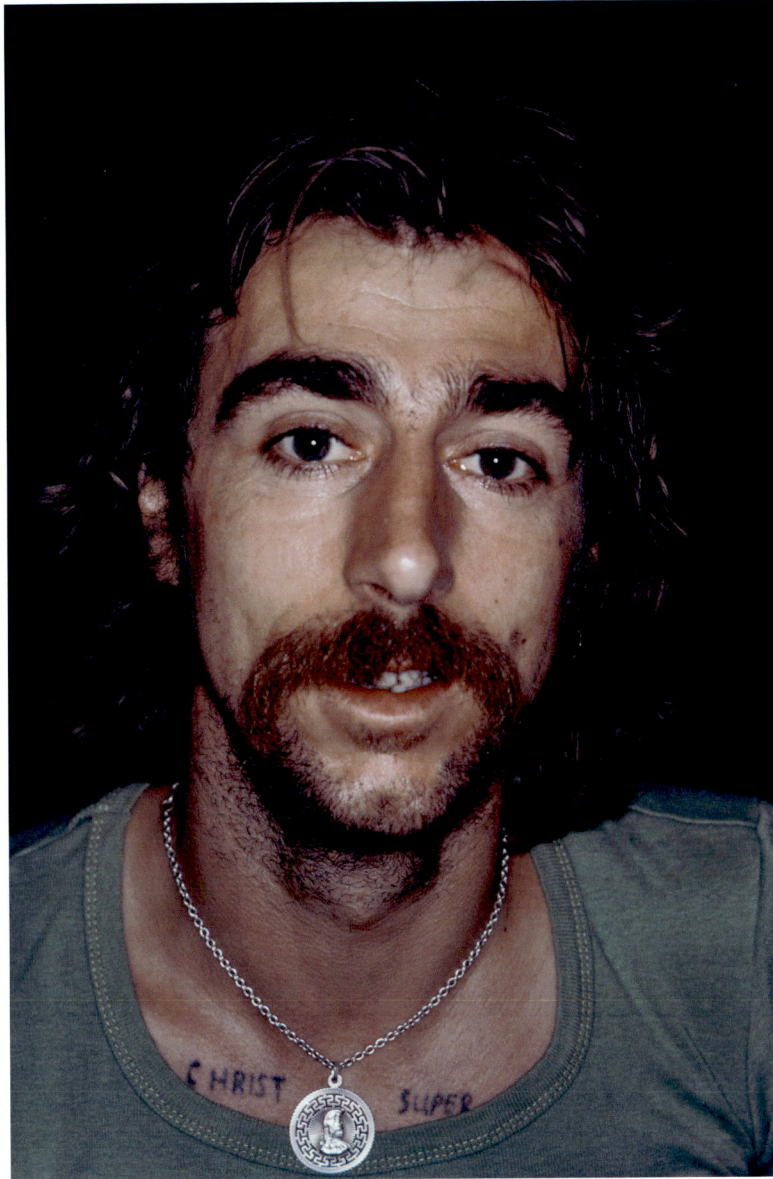

Paddy

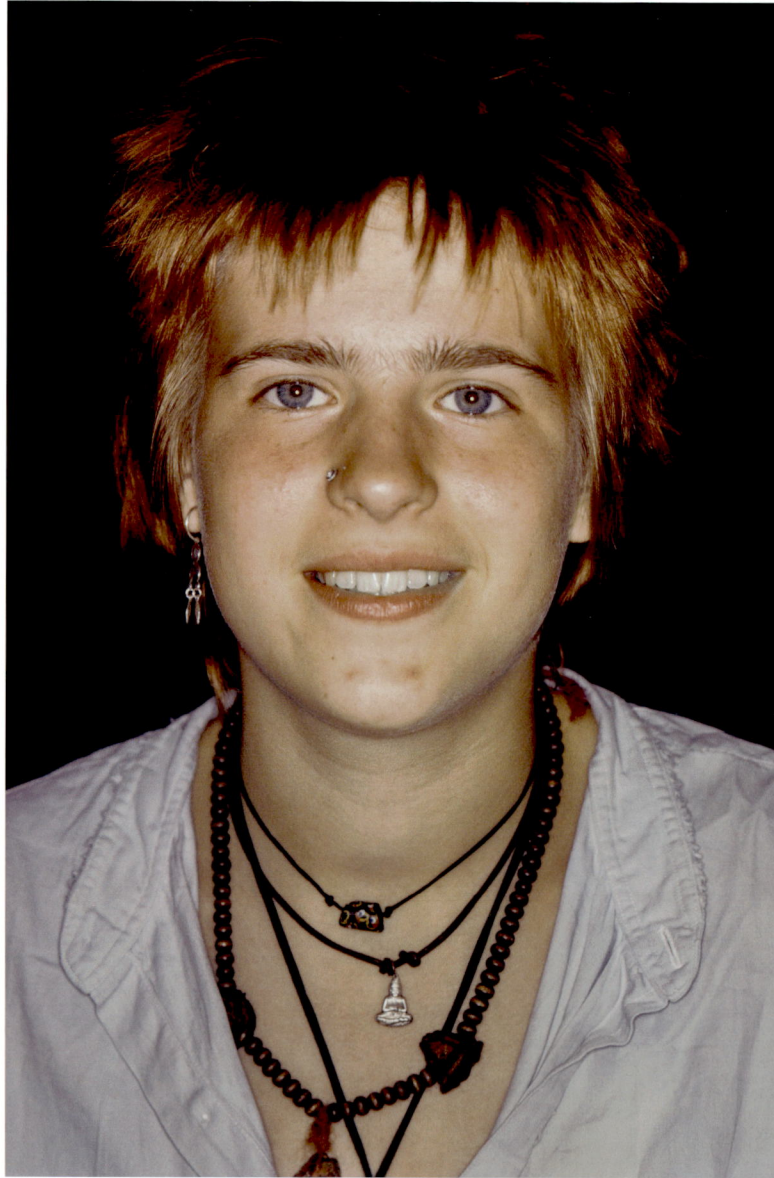

Susana

Emerich

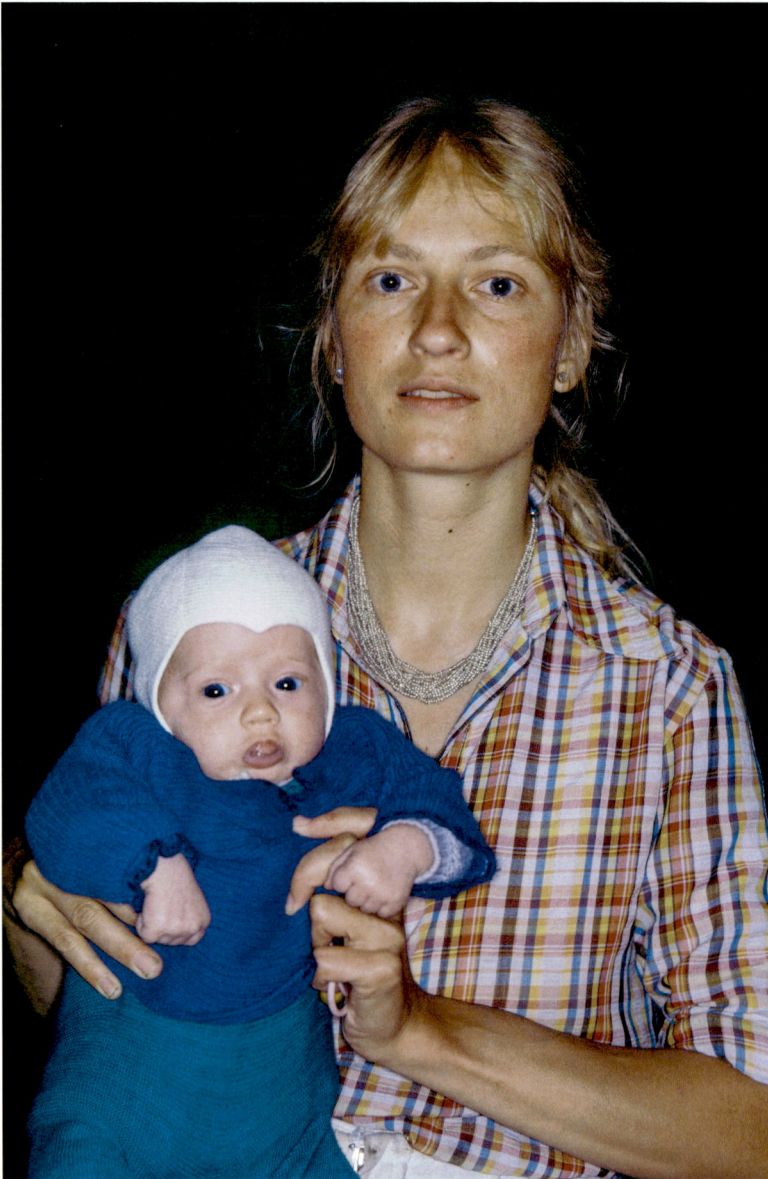

Helle   Sonja

Jesper   Marie   Lise

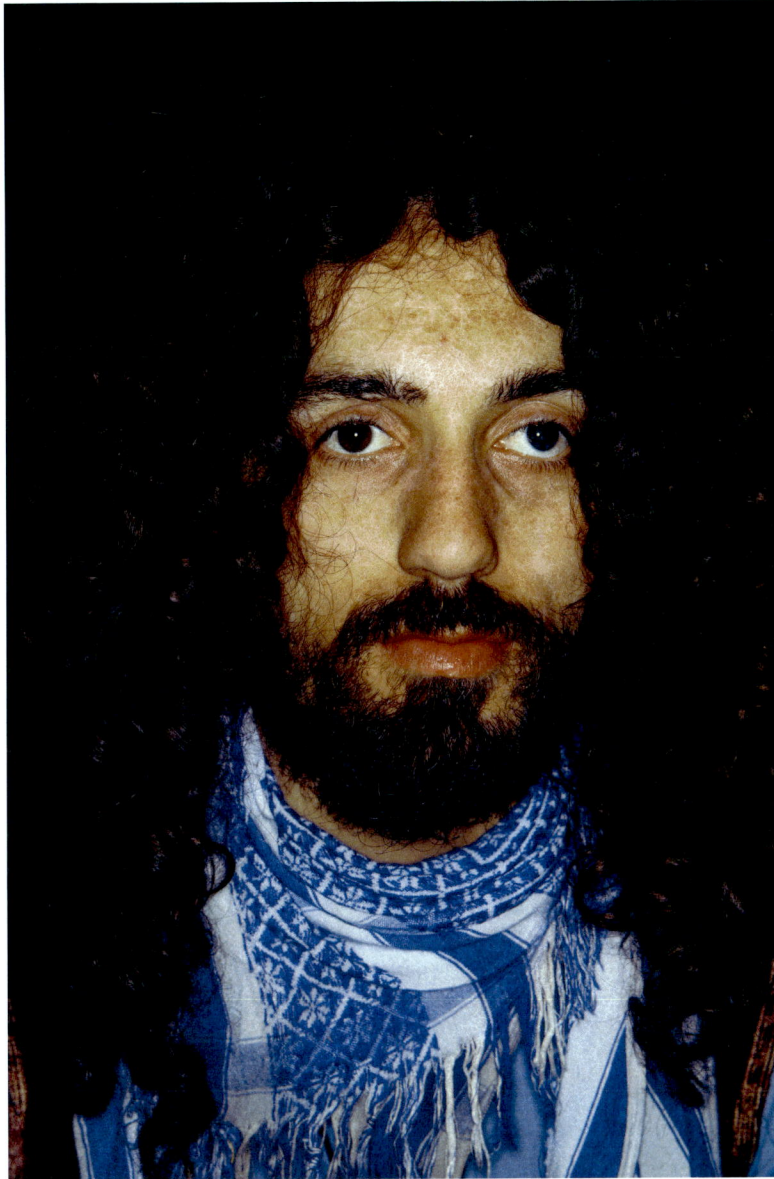

Charlie

# WORK

Christiania provides the economic environment right-wing businessmen dream of—virtually no rules or regulations, no bureaucracy and almost no tax. Apart from the hash pushers, who are a law unto themselves, Christianites have used this freedom to establish collectively run workshops. The Freetown business model combines features that both appeal to and repel left-and right-wing supporters, leaving both sides of the political divide uneasy.

At their best, these workshops provide Christianites with a second family. Work is done at a pre-industrial pace and children particularly love seeing how things are made. The 'workers' have the opportunity to connect with the wider community through products tailored to its lifestyle.

Every Sunday at four o'clock we have a meeting. We all walk round the bakery, writing down everything we need to order for the next week. (I must order this week and I have forgotten, so I must do that tomorrow…) We check that we have enough money to buy everything we need, and if we have any money left over, we buy extra ingredients, like whole-wheat or sesame seeds, to add to the bread. When that's done, we draw up a rota for the coming week, so that everyone can work at least one shift, and maybe once a month get a chance to bake twice.

Every day we make six batches of dough and from each batch we get thirty-five loaves. Usually we make about two hundred loaves, a hundred and fifty rolls and twenty baguettes a day. It takes two people working in the bakery to make that much bread each night. In winter we make much less, about one hundred and fifty loaves. Altogether we bake about half the bread that is eaten in Christiania. We make a special bread for Fælleskøkkenet (the community kitchen), and for Woodstock. Some of the bread we make is sold here in the bakery, but most of it's sold in Indkøbscentralen (the general store) and Grønsagen (the greengrocers). We sell the loaves to the shops for 5 Kr. (50p) and they sell them for 5.50 Kr. We divide the money so that 2.50 Kr. goes to the bakers and 2.50 Kr. goes to the bakery for ingredients and equipment.

Usually the bakers get about 300 Kr. (£30) a night, but sometimes it's a bit more. If you're baking on Saturday, for example, there are a lot of tourists, so you can sell more bread directly.

If people in our collective don't have money they are looked after by the bakery and they can always eat in here—there is always food.

One girl had to go to Germany yesterday, and she only had enough money for the train. She had no other money at all, so she took some from the bakery account. She went to help someone from Christiania who was in trouble, so of course she could take it. Another guy badly needed money; he told us that if he didn't pay what he owed, he would have to go to prison. We let him work by himself in the bakery one night, so he got all the money from that night's shift. So, if people really need money, they can earn it in the bakery, or they can take it from our account.

It's a working collective; we don't live together. Our common concern is the bakery and looking after it. A short time ago, one guy who worked here tried to run the bakery as if he were the boss, and there was a very, very bad vibe. He would come in every morning to inspect the bread and make sure that the place was clean. He controlled everything and wouldn't even let us know where the flour came from, or how much money we had in the capital fund. No one else knew how the bakery worked. So, we had a 'revolution' to kick him out. That meant that we had to find out how to run everything ourselves. Now that we know, it's not so difficult. It's much nicer working in a place where you understand the whole process, where you're not just one cog in a machine.

We're now saving for a new oven, because the one we have doesn't cook evenly. I can tell just by looking at the bread in the shop which shelf it was cooked on and which baker made it! Wolfgang's bread is always flat because he keeps it in the steam box too long. He drinks too much, so he forgets to take.it out at the right time. Anja is an experienced baker, and her bread is always very, very good. If you buy bread and you find pieces of flour in it, it may mean that it was made by the young German girls, because they mix the bread in the pot instead of on the table. They're a bit lazy—it's very difficult to mix good dough in these pots. Then there's Keeps—when he's baking, he always puts something funny on top of the bread. But his bread is very good, even though he started baking only recently.

If you wanted to join the collective, you'd have to come by for a couple of weeks, and for the first two or three days just talk to people. Then you might start to help with cleaning, but not in the bakery itself—you'd do the garden. You might say, 'What a nice vibe you have here,' and then bring a few cigarettes, and come and watch us make the bread. Then you'd ask if there were enough people, or if anybody was sick. There might be a day when extra help is needed, and if there was, you could say, 'Maybe I could come and help. I'm not bothered about being paid, I just want to work.' If they replied, 'No, we don't need anyone right now', you'd have to smile and show that everything was okay, and keep at it, and eventually, if you were lucky, you'd get put on the list.

We make bread and we entertain the tourists! Many come along and watch. The children especially are fascinated to see how the bread's made, because they don't have the chance to do that in town. Lots of people from Christiania call in during the night for a coffee and a chat. It's very nice to have company when you're baking.

# THE POSTMAN—BILL

Post for Christiania was delivered to one address by the post office. It was reliably sorted and delivered by Christianites each day. Christiania's dogs shared the universal dislike of postmen. Here, Bill has to negotiate not just angry dogs, but geese as well.

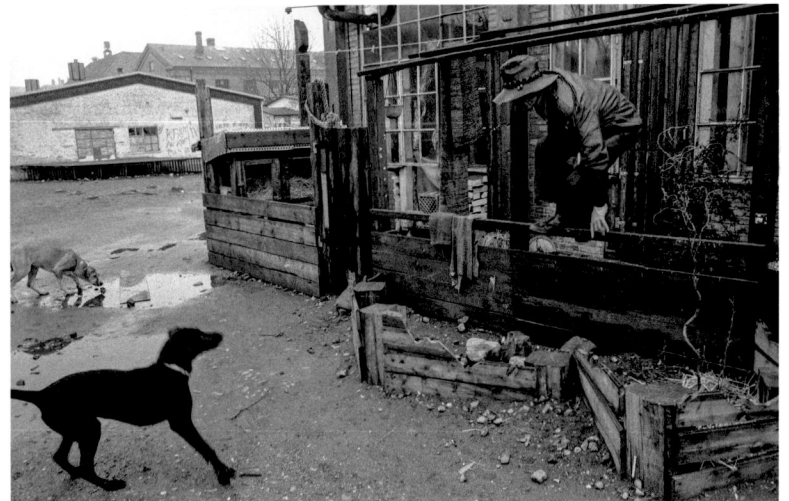

*Michael makes his candles by threading string between hooks on a metal basket. There are four baskets hanging from beams. They are pivoted so that each one can be suspended above a barrel of candle wax, already heated to the correct temperature, and then dipped. A thin layer of wax is added each time the basket is dipped until the candle is the correct size.*

*One of the most important discoveries of nineteenth-century candle-making was the self-trimming wick, which we now take completely for granted. An additional thin piece of cord is bound into the string, which has the effect of turning the wick over in a loop, which stops the flame burning too quickly. This simple device put thousands of people who had been employed to trim candles out of work. Not many people know that.*

*Michael can make up to four thousand candles a week—'enough to feed four people and two dogs,' he said. While I photographed him making the candles, he talked about the runaway children who come to Christiania.*

Only two of the twelve kids who were staying here recently are living here now. The others lived here for some months, but the first thing we do is contact their parents. They are usually quite upset—because it's Christiania and that name suggests all kinds of things to them—but many of the girls would've ended up in Vesterbro as prostitutes if they hadn't come here. Sometimes we go to Vesterbro and pick them up, but they all come here sooner or later.

All the children here recently, except one, came from the Copenhagen suburbs, mostly from homes where there was no family life, where their parents drank or fought. Christiania is a place where they come and say, 'Help, I need food and attention.'

*How do they know where to go?*

They don't know what to do—they sit around in bars like Woodstock. If they talk to a Christianite, he or she will tell them they can stay in Multimedia House for a night and then talk to Bent, who will find a place for them to stay temporarily while he contacts the authorities.

*How many kids come to Christiania in a year?*

In a year, I would say about a hundred. I know from Bent, that since '73 we have had about six hundred children coming through Christiania. They just want to get away from the trouble at home.

*Do you plan to stay in Christiania?*

Yes, I think I'll stay for another year, and then go travelling, either by boat or jeep, I don't quite know. I want to travel with a group, for a year, and then maybe come home and settle down—somewhere in Scandinavia, somewhere in the country, I think. And then live by fishing, hunting and farming, and have some children.

*In many ways Christiania is like a pre-industrial community, isn't it?*

Yes, but I don't believe that Christiania is an end station—it's more like a step towards something else. You get to know people here, and you work together in a different way. I believe that Christiania should stay like that—there's a great need for it in Copenhagen and in all big cities. It has a very important social function.

## JØRGEN'S ELEPHANTS

I'd been in the Månefiskeren, one of Christiania's extraordinary bars, and decided to go out for a breath of fresh air.

Jørgen was outside and we talked. After a few moments he said, 'Well, I must go back to work.' 'What do you mean? You've never worked in your life!' 'I'll go and do a bit of "take it easy, take it easy"—I'll show you.'

We went back inside and Jørgen strode up to a couple of strangers. He put on his most menacing expression and started rolling up his shirt sleeves, then his trousers. He had a petticoat wrapped around his head. A black eye, the result of a dispute the night before, coloured his face. The strangers froze. For a few minutes, they struggled to continue some kind of conversation. Jørgen flexed his muscles and demanded in a loud, threatening voice that they immediately return his elephants. 'I have four elephants—I know you stole them, and I want them back—NOW.' He kicked a chair to emphasise the point.

Barney—it was always Barney, the self-styled keeper of the peace—appeared from nowhere and came over to calm Jørgen down. 'Okay, take it easy, take it easy, forget about your elephants.' Jørgen shook hands with the strangers, with Barney, with me and the people at the next table whose dogs were barking at us. 'You see, Mark, I do a little "take it easy, take it easy", and they freak out—I don't know why—I'm just doing my job.'

The next day we met by chance in Christianshavn. 'Mark, have you got your camera?' I had. 'Okay, wait there.' He stopped a taxi, told me to get in, took a piss, and then climbed in too.

He told the driver to take us to Benneweis Circus. I followed Jørgen through a big iron door and along a passage to a room in which there were five elephants. They clearly recognised him; one by one they reached out their trunks and touched his face, leaving circles of wetness around his mouth.

'Have you got the pictures? Good. I shall want copies, Mark. I've been telling them in Christiania for years that I have my elephants. No one believes me—I don't know why.' He looked very serious, then started to laugh at himself.

## THE SMITHY—JESPER

The Smithy first started at Autogena [one of the buildings in Dyssen, on the far side of the lake]. Rene, Spacy and me were living there. We had no electricity, but we did a lot of experimenting. First, we designed a bicycle trailer and an oil-drum stove for burning wood. We were trying to design technology to suit the Christiania lifestyle.

Our first stoves were fairly primitive. They were based on an article I had read about how to make a wood-burning stove without welding, just using a hammer and chisel and an empty oil drum. You see, most people were heating their rooms with oil stoves, which was expensive. The wood-burning stoves became popular because free wood was delivered to Christiania by the guys demolishing old houses in town.

In 1973 we moved to this big workshop. We'd been making stoves for a year. We also collected old metal for scrap and made a living out of selling the big old boilers used to heat Christiania when it was an army base. They were already broken, so we just had to cut them up. It was a fun way of making a living.

At that time, about 90 per cent of our products were sold in Christiania. Then, after moving to this big workshop, we tried—and succeeded—in making things for people outside Christiania as well, and that's what we're doing today. Now more than 90 per cent of the things we make are for outside, for export. We make about twenty stoves a month, but the cycle trailers are our biggest sellers—we've made five hundred this year [1977].

We have to make over 35,000 Kr. (£3,500) a month—if we made less than 30,000, we'd go bust. We record everything in a cash book, wages and expenses, and we take turns in being cashier. We don't use the book for anything else—we don't pay taxes or have to show it to anyone—but it's become a ritual. However, the smithy is starting to change now because we've decided to apply for a tax number, and we also have a bank account. We all get the same pay. My wage is now 525 Kr. (£52) a week, sometimes less, never more, but we also get a lot of other things—facilities, food, clothes, a lot of things. In Christiania we're rich.

And the work's not too rigid. If you take a day's holiday, you don't get paid for it, but if you're sick, you do. And if you're very poor, we pay other bills for you. We paid Bernt's dentist's bill of 200 Kr. for instance, and we ought to do more of that sort of thing, so that the workshop provides real security for its members.

Preben at work in the smithy

A lot of people are rich in this way in Christiania. Normally, single people tend to be poor and lonely; it's much better when seven or eight work together. There are about twenty such 'families' in Christiania, and they're a good thing—people love each other and help each other. But none of these families are allowed to get too much power. For instance, when the Blue House tried to organise how Christiania was run, other families stepped in to stop them. I have seen Fabrikken do this too; when one family tries to organise everything, the others close ranks.

One thing you might be interested to know is that we are going to stop restoring old machinery and reusing materials. Making the oil-drum stoves is dangerous work, because of the poisonous fumes. Before one can be used, we have to burn them out to get rid of all the deposits. It's dirty work—you have to be crazy to do it. We even got some drums from a chemical factory—we had no idea what was in them. So, we've stopped recycling materials, and are using new iron instead, which is much easier to cut and not too expensive. It was a nice idea to recycle the old oil and water tanks to make stoves, but in practice it was very unpleasant.

Christiania is not exactly an alternative, it's more an attempt to move the borders of our society further out. In the smithy, we're living on the border, and we're trying to extend the border of what can be done. We made five hundred cycle trailers last year; this year we will make a thousand—and that's a lot of work, a lot of money.

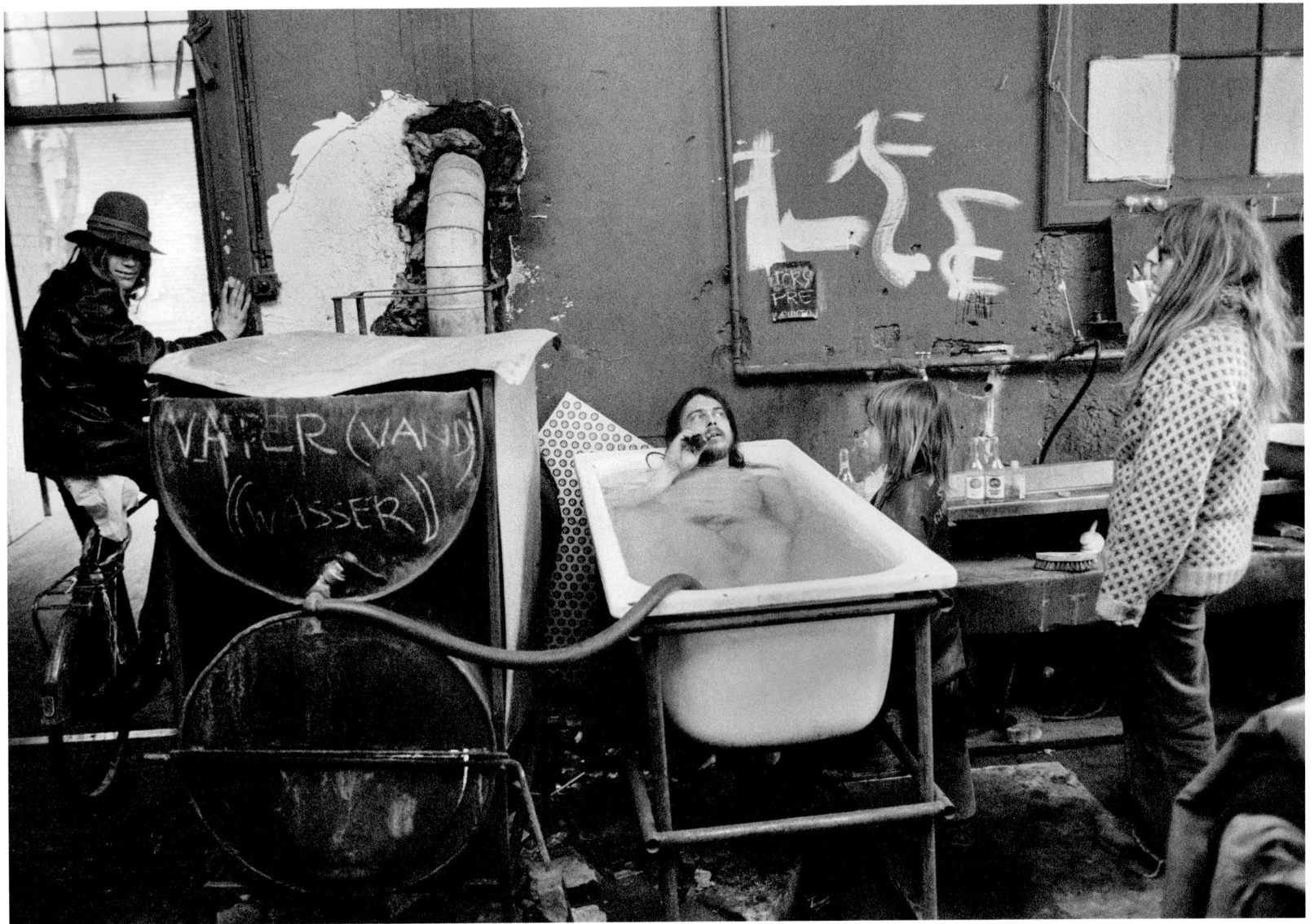

VATER (VAND)
((WISSER))

## THE HEALTH HOUSE—STEEN

Christiania has its special health problems and its own remedies. In summer, a lot of people come to us with cut feet because there's so much broken glass around. Of course, if it's a bad cut, we call an ambulance immediately, and if an ambulance won't come, we get a taxi. Sometimes doctors and ambulances refuse to come to Christiania— they just don't dare to—so one of our jobs is to act as a go-between for doctors and ill people. It might mean taking someone to the street outside and waiting until he or she is collected.

Another problem is staphylococcus, but not the really serious kind people get in hospital, which is extremely difficult to get rid of because it has developed in an environment where antibiotics are frequently present. Nevertheless, the Christiania version is troublesome and this is where herbal remedies come in. Lice and fleas aren't much of a problem, or at least if they are, people treat themselves.

You might be interested to know that we get quite a few people coming to us suffering from stress. They're very nervous, unable to sleep and sometimes they think they are being followed by the police. Well, we give them herbal tranquillisers, which are not as strong as the chemical ones but have a similar effect. But we also talk with people for hours—going through their daily routine, finding out how much they sleep, what they eat and what problems they have. They might need help to find a more comfortable room, or to move away from Christiania, or to stop breaking the law if that's their problem.

Then there are people with nutritional problems. We advise them to include more vegetables in their diet. We help them learn how to cure themselves.

We mostly use herbal remedies but if people's problems do not respond to them, we of course use chemical medicines. We always ask people who we think will respond to herbal medicine if they want to try our approach and explain carefully what the advantages of both treatments are. Penicillin, for example, will cure you very quickly but will not be so effective next time. Nor does it help your body fight the illness; it does it for you, so it makes your body lazy.

But in a lot of cases, if you know what you are doing you can use chemical medicines. The problem is, they don't help your body build its own resistance. This approach to treatment, helping the body get well, is undeveloped in Western medicines. Herbal medicines don't become less effective with use but generally take longer, demanding more energy from your own body and more attention from the patient.

Obviously, we don't ask anyone who is seriously ill and who clearly needs a course of antibiotics if they want a herbal cure. Nor do we ask people who smoke a lot of hash or drink a lot. For one thing, we can't be sure they'll return for the next treatment, which is very important with herbal cures, and we have also found that people who smoke a lot of hash have fewer white blood cells (the cells that fight infection). So, in these cases herbal treatment isn't so effective.

Twice a year, all the Health House workers go to gather herbs in the countryside. The herbs you collect yourself are the best but of course there are many herbs that don't grow in Denmark and we have to buy them.

With some problems, we can only treat the symptoms. For example, if you have toothache, oil of cloves will take away the pain, but you still have the underlying problem—you still have to go to a dentist. You can get rid of a stress headache with an oil massage and there are plenty of herbal medicines with pain-relieving properties. Hops used for making beer contain a substance which is similar to the active ingredient in aspirin, as does camomile, the flower used in herbal tea. But if you have someone who is screaming with pain you don't start brewing up camomile tea—you give them a pill.

We treat symptoms of course, but our aim is always to get the patient to see his headache as a signal to change. That's what we aim to do in the Health House—to find out what is really wrong.

We open three days a week from three o'clock to six o'clock. Between five and ten people work here. None of us are qualified doctors, nor do we get paid. The common fund provides some money for us and the Indkøbscentralen (the general store) is very generous. There are collection boxes in the shops and restaurants and a collection box on the table in the Health House, but these donations provide only a small part of our income.

People need to learn a bit more about their bodies. And society needs 'street' doctors. Not people who have trained for years, but people who work like us, with some knowledge of herbs. Every street should have a Health House, something between the accident and the hospital, so to speak. The practice we have developed in the Health House could be replicated in society at large very easily. A lot of people, including doctors from Copenhagen, have taken a great deal of interest in our work here. We even have a few patients from Copenhagen visiting us for treatment.

## THE KINDERGARTEN—PER AND VIBEKE

Per: Initially the kindergarten was not recognised by the authorities, and that was how we wanted it. The parents ran it without state funding, donating their time, food, materials and money, if they were able to. The government couldn't impose their regulations and it ran very well—better than many of the state kindergartens. So then the authorities became interested.

Vibeke: Three lawyers from the Ministry of Social Welfare contacted us and said they wanted us to write a paper about the place. We told them they could come and stay as long as they wanted, but that they would have to write their own paper. We didn't want to fix the kindergarten on a piece of paper—it was developing all the time… Anyway, they decided that the kindergarten was okay, and that they didn't need to interfere, and that was when our problems began.

From then on it became possible for parents to get benefits to keep their children in our kindergarten. So, one girl who was out of work decided to apply for benefit payments for her child, and soon after that everybody else started to do the same. I think we were the only two who didn't. It became an institution. The children went to the kindergarten for the day and the parents did something else. Recently, we had to close it for a time because parents couldn't even be bothered to collect the money from the social welfare office!

What we'd dreamed of was a place where the children could play, with a workshop where they could help us make soap, toothpaste and other simple things, if they wanted. We hoped to sell these things through Indkøbscentralen (the general store). We didn't want an institution where the kids would be left all day with someone else—you can do that anywhere.

Per: Social welfare has poisoned people. At first, we were united in Christiania in not seeking help. We wanted to really live outside the system, but it seems to be too big a temptation for most people—and when they get the money they are 'independent' in the worst way. It destroyed the community feeling in Christiania.

*Mr. X is a nervous, slick young man with many facts at his fingertips. He could have made quick profits on the Stock Exchange but fate took him to Christiania, where his considerable talents in the import business have helped to keep supplies of dope moving into the Freetown.*

My impression is that Christiania supplies up to 15 per cent of the dope that is smoked in Denmark. There's always dope here, but Christiania isn't the main dope centre in Denmark. Nor is dope being smuggled into the rest of Denmark by people from Christiania. It's a distribution centre, and it costs about 2 Kr. (20p) a gram more in Christiania than elsewhere.

At the moment, when times are good and supplies meet demand, about one tenth of the people in Christiania are dealing—around 100 people. But a lot of the dealers are just opportunists—they make 40-50 Kr. (£4-5) a day. A street pusher, one of the professional, hard-working street pushers, who can give a personal guarantee that the hash is of good quality, could move anywhere between 300g and 2kg. There are also a few pushers who sell to other smaller dealers. Pushers can avoid coming into conflict with the police for a long time. The less greedy they are, the safer they are. Most pushers are more interested in dealing hash than making lots of money. They make an average of 1.25-1.50 Kr. a gram, so some evenings they may be able to earn 200-300 Kr., but there are overheads. They might smoke 5-10g themselves a day and at Woodstock many of them will hand out 10-20 Kr. a day to people who can't afford to buy cigarettes or food. Or they might buy a round of beer or cigarettes. These are all overheads and are expected. There's an unwritten law on Pusher Street that if you ask someone for a beer or cigarette, they'll give it to you. It costs you just to be on Pusher Street. There are very few people getting rich, very few making enough money to save for the future, to buy a house in the country, say, or move to Morocco, or buy a shop in town.

The unwritten laws that govern Pusher Street are quite strict. It's very difficult to come into Christiania from outside and start selling dope. You'd have to do it discreetly and slowly build up your reputation.

You have two kinds of pushers, the smoking pushers, who understand how to smoke, and the ones who see it as a job, a way to make an easy living. The dealers around the main entrance are mainly junkies. For them, selling hash in Christiania is the easiest way to get the money they need for their fix. In any case, it's better they do that than rip off shops, break into homes or prostitute themselves. The other people in Christiania tolerate them and sometimes try to help them get off junk, by engaging with them, talking to them. Some organisations based in Copenhagen, such as Club 47, also come here to talk to them and help them kick the habit. One of the unwritten rules of Christiania is that junk is not to be sold here, because the resulting paranoia, thefts, break-ins and general bad vibes would destroy the place. That's what's happened in San Francisco, London and other places where it's been allowed to spread.

Very few of the pushers in Christiania have access to large amounts of dope because the big dealers don't want to know them. So, they have to make do with a 100-gram man, who'll maybe give them 30 to 40 grams to work with, although you sometimes find a few dealers with as much as a quarter of a kilo. The people around Woodstock tend to have larger quantities because it's a more difficult place to bust. It's easy to see the police approaching Woodstock because it's right in the middle of Christiania—people can slip away. There are a lot of different escape routes.

Christiania was actually founded by two groups of people: the squatters (they weren't squatting for political reasons; they really needed a place to live) and the dope dealers. In the beginning it was like the Wild West here, very rough and hard. Very few people came here and there was nothing about it in the media.

In 1971, in the aftermath of the youth rebellion, dope was a new thing, but spreading very fast. In 1967, there were four people working in Narcotics in the Copenhagen Police Department, basically just overseeing the registration of addicts. They didn't know anything about hash or marihuana. I remember the first bust in Copenhagen—they found 3kg in a cellar in Christianshavn. The man who had it got four months in prison. In 1970, after the World Bank demonstration, the police formed the Uro Patrol. They're in plain clothes—that's their fancy dress. They try to blend in, but you easily spot them by their eyes and their build—they're usually very strong and healthy-looking.

The Uro Patrol are interested in getting the big dealers, but they can't make mistakes, because the bigger dealers have connections, and if the Uros find nothing, there would be a huge stink about it. The small dealers provide some kind of justification for the Uro Patrol coming into the area.

But the hash laws are a big problem for the authorities because they can't just fill up all the jails with dealers. The law in Denmark is that all narcotics, including hash, are illegal, but the authorities are aware that a lot is being smoked all over Denmark every day, so there's an informal attitude towards the possession of marihuana. You can have up to 30, even 40, kroner's worth (£3-4) in your possession, and although they may confiscate it and maybe fine you, they will not jail you—it would cost them 200-300 Kr. (£20-30) a day to keep you in jail. In any case dealers who end up in jail carry on selling hash there.

There are always rumours that the police have spies living in Christiania, but if such a person lived here for just a few months, he could bust the whole place. And not much would come out of it. It's a kind of Sisyphean struggle. They can't get rid of dope by busting the dealers or the smokers.

The first rule between the people on Pusher Street is honesty. That's the basic rule for survival because anything said on Pusher Street can be checked. If you are dishonest, you won't last more than a week, sometimes only an hour or two. Pushers have to be honest with each other and their customers. They can play games, they can bicker about whose spot it is, but never about anything serious… There are 'hearings' almost every day about who has the right to be in a particular place, and a majority verdict is reached very quickly—it never takes long. Conflict on Pusher Street can't last for more than five minutes without disrupting the whole set-up. It's an edgy business to begin with, so the cooler, the more together, the more mass-protective you get, the better off you are. Another unwritten law makes it very difficult for foreigners to push on Pusher Street, firstly because the other Christianites are suspicious of them, and secondly because they are easier for the police to bust. But

there are other laws too—it's all a question of survival, right? Mutual *fælleskab*—mutual community.

Lots of people say that the pushers don't contribute anything, but that's not true. They do contribute, but there are problems. Sometimes, when there are too many of them on Pusher Street, they really do start to 'push'—yelling, falling over people to sell dope—it can get a bit tense at times. But what they do contribute is security, the security of fulfilling other people's needs for dope. And you know it's professional work—when I smoke, well, I like to buy my dope from someone who also smokes and is into dope culture.

Hash dealers operating near the old entrance to Christiania.

144　Woodstock. A café with more to offer than coffee and sandwiches.

## ON THE BOAT TO GOA...

A few years after *Christiania* was published, I met one of the smugglers who supplied Christiania's dealers with hash. I was on the boat from Bombay (now Mumbai) to Goa, keeping a friend company as he searched for his girlfriend. He'd split up with her in Goa a few months earlier. Back in London he started to miss her. So, here we were, sitting on the deck of the steamer that ferried passengers up and down India's west coast. Just before it left the docks, we saw a tall, blond guy get on the boat. You couldn't miss him—he was handcuffed to an Indian man. They made their way over to us and sat down. Despite being chained to each other there was no acknowledgement that they were travelling together. The Indian guy sat looking away from us and as far from his companion as his tether would allow.

Socially this was a difficult situation, but before my friend or I had a chance to speak, the blond guy looked at me and said: 'I know who you are; I saw you in Christiania. You were making a book. I supply at least a quarter of the hash sold there. We had a lot of discussion about you—were you really working for the police, or just making a book? Should we let you photograph Woodstock and the hash dealers? In the end it was decided you were okay. The dealers felt that they were part of Christiania and that they should be included in the book. I wasn't convinced.'

He had a cold, military air about him. He made no attempt to be friendly, but of course we were curious to know why he was handcuffed to his companion. In the end I asked what the story was. 'Okay. I'll tell you,' he said. 'He was a beggar, sitting outside the Taj Hotel[9] in Bombay. I took him off the streets, smuggled him into my room at the Taj; got a barber to cut his hair; got a tailor to make clothes for him. He shared my life—he had the best of everything: pink Champagne, wonderful food—he lived like a prince. I took him with me to Goa when I went to meet the guys I buy hash from.

'When we got to Goa, I hired a motorbike. I crashed on the first trip—I couldn't make a corner on the road between Panjim and Mapusa.[10] I hit two boulders at the side of the road. Just before I crashed, I thought, "Now, I'm going to find out what it's like to fly." I went over the handlebars, somersaulted once, perhaps twice, and landed on my back twenty metres away. I was unconscious. When I woke up in hospital my money for the deal was gone, $20,000 (about

9    The Taj Mahal Palace is a five-star hotel by India Gate in Mumbai.

10   Panjim, now known as Panaji, is the capital of Goa state. Mapusa is a town in northern Goa.

$60,000 in today's money). I knew immediately what had happened. This guy,' he said, pointing at the Indian, 'had gone to the dealers and told them I was in hospital. I was sure they'd told him to steal the money and bring it to them. I guessed they'd told him they'd split it with him if he did—and kill him if he didn't. Turned out I was right.

'As soon as I was okay to leave hospital, I set out to find him. It took me six months! I tracked him down—one guy out of 60 million people. I got him on this boat so I could take him to the dealers and confront them.

'Well, I made a mistake. I fell asleep and he jumped overboard and swam to the shore. It took me another three months to find him. This time he won't get away. This time I will get my money back and then I'll kill the dealers. I'll cut them to pieces with a machete.'

We were afloat on the Arabian Sea listening to what sounded like a modern version of *The Book of the Thousand Nights and One Night*.[11] But this wasn't a flight of the imagination; we were listening to a very determined, violent man talking about murder. We suggested alternative ways to solve the problem without killing people, but he wouldn't listen. 'I don't care about the money,' he said. 'I was insured—I got the money back already. But I don't like being cheated—I won't be cheated.'

We said goodbye when we docked at Panjim. I have no idea what happened to him, or the dealers, or his unwilling companion. Real-life travellers' tales often lack proper endings. We found a cheap hotel and next day we walked along the beach. A sea mist had rolled in—you couldn't see more than a few metres. Suddenly Bo (or Kim), one of the twins in the picture on page 84, appeared, walking towards me. 'Good God,' he said. 'Mark, I can't believe it's you. I just sent a telegram to a friend in Christiania, asking for a copy of the photo you took of us outside the Dome house. I've run out of money and was going to print it on T-shirts and sell them to the freaks on the beach. And now here you are.'

He told us about his strange adventures in India, but at this point I'll take a leaf out of Scheherazade's story book and 'fall discreetly silent'. Except to say that we did find my friend's lover. She was living with two guys in a bungalow by the beach, so the hoped-for reconciliation didn't happen. Another example of a traveller's tale without a proper ending.

---

11  The Book of the Thousand Nights and One Night, often known in English as The Arabian Nights, is a collection of folk tales collected over many centuries by scholars across Asia and North Africa. There are many versions, including a new English translation published by Penguin Classics. To read it is to be transported back to ancient eastern folklore and literature, a world of magic and mystery far beyond the imagination of today's storytellers. From the epic adventures of 'Aladdin and the Enchanted Lamp' to the farcical 'Young Woman and her Five Lovers' and the social criticism of 'The Tale of the Hunchback', the stories depict a fabulous world of all-powerful sorcerers, jinns imprisoned in bottles and enchanting princesses.

## COPS AND DEALERS

Police raids were an occasional feature of life in Christiania but loomed large in the collective imagination. The police came in like cowboys to a reservation and provoked an angry response from some Christianites. This in turn provoked an even stronger response from the police. Here we see our tribal natures in full flood.

# LAURIE GRUNDT

*Some people pretend to be artists; they pull out sketchpads and easels, hoping to be watched and admired. Laurie never did that. He took you into his world to share his political commitments and his passion for beauty. So here he is, quietly working away in his studio, not needing to prove anything to anybody. Laurie died on the 1st January 2020.*

*Do you prefer living here to living in a community of artists?*

I like it here—it's been good for me. One of the great things about Christiania is that when I feel tired or a bit mad, I can go out without worrying that someone will make me feel ridiculous, because there are so many ridiculous people here already. I like that about the place.

I don't believe in 'café society', I believe in workshops. I've never spent much time in cafés. Happiness comes from making things and observing life. I hate all the drugs that make it impossible to coordinate or synchronise your movements and thoughts. How the hell can you achieve anything when you're lying on the floor smoking hash all day? It's just an excuse for the Uro Patrol to come nosing around. They should be looking for drugs, but they don't help Christiania get rid of them, because they want to keep some of the self-destruction alive. I know they're provoked at times in Christiania, but they don't approach it in the right way. All they seem to do is go after poor people. If they see someone who isn't well dressed, they immediately think that he's suspicious. So, they've never managed to build up any kind of friendly relations with the community.

I hate all kinds of drugs, except perhaps a bit of hash from time to time, for the feeling of peace it gives…

There should be more workshops in Christiania, where people could go to do things, learn things, and to talk. Their restless fingers would then be occupied and become creative. Creative people are beautiful people, because they are mentally relaxed. They've put away their ambitions, and if you feel sad or lonely, they just let you feel that way and help you ease the pressure.

*I can see you're interested in communism. Have you travelled in communist countries?*

Not much, just as a tourist. I like their drinks, and their dreams of Lenin and Trotsky. But I think the best system is here in Christiania, where everybody has to learn to trust themselves, and is free to raise their voices without fears of repression. That was the real dream of Lenin and Trotsky—to create a society in which everyone could voice their opinion.

But then it was taken over by a central committee, one that was beyond criticism—that was the tragedy.

Christiania has got a lot of things right. When I walk around, and see the hard-working, politically engaged people in Fabrikken, in Information, working from morning to evening, I feel a bit ashamed that I haven't joined them, to write manifestos and work to help others.

*What surprises me about the artists in Christiania is that they don't paint or draw the wonderful faces and the extraordinary life you see all around. We're living in a so-called social experiment but the social experiments you're painting are political experiments taking place outside Christiania.*

You're doing it—you're doing that job. I just couldn't—I would like to do it, but I can't. I get too nervous.

*For many years, Christiania had its own internationally acclaimed theatre group, Solvognen. The group staged ambitious musicals in the Grey Hall, playing to packed audiences, as well as highly original agitprop street theatre performances in Copenhagen and Sweden.*

*How did Solvognen start?*

It started as a lightshow in 1969 with just four people. Gradually, they became more interested in theatre and were joined by actors from Copenhagen's Underground Theatre. Their first performance was in October 1972, at a big demonstration—around 19,000 people protesting against Denmark joining the EEC [now the EU].

During the next year, Solvognen produced nearly twenty plays, the best known of which was the one about the NATO army, which they performed during the 1973 meeting of the NATO Council of Ministers in Copenhagen. By this time, many members of Solvognen had moved to Christiania, and we decided to make it our base. There was a lot of space for rehearsals—the Grey Hall was wonderful for big productions, with room for over a thousand people. There were also workshops and a flea market where we could buy props. It was perfect.

For the NATO play we hired military tents and got into our roles by imposing strict military discipline on the group. Everyone had to wear immaculate uniforms, turn up on time and behave like disciplined soldiers. Every day there were events in the streets of Copenhagen. People couldn't tell if we were actors or NATO soldiers. It led to some really funny moments: at one point two real policemen were arrested by two military policemen who thought they were Solvognen actors. The civilian police then attempted to arrest the military police, believing them to be Solvognen actors trying to make trouble. The biggest performance, lasting seven hours, was a cabaret with a satirical take on the Cold War. It was held in the Grey Hall and the audience had to participate and act as if they were pro-NATO. They were a key part of the performance. It was the most powerful theatrical experience I have ever had.

*Does Solvognen function as a cooperative?*

There's a core group of about thirty people who attend monthly meetings where we discuss ideas, but there are many others who help from time to time. It's kind of anarchical in the way it works. We believe that everyone in the group should act, as well as take part in the practical work, such as sewing costumes and making props. We're against the idea of people having set roles, for example only taking care of the lights, or the administration or the typing.

*How does it work financially? Do you use the money you make from ticket sales to pay wages?*

Well, I think this is the first time we've tried to pay some kind of wage to people who don't have any other source of income. They get the equivalent of between five and ten pounds a day. When a play makes money, we normally invest it in equipment—the tent we perform in, for instance, or lighting or sound equipment. Some money goes towards the street actions as well. Generally, we don't make much money, because we keep the ticket prices as low as possible— it works out cheaper to see both the plays we're putting on at the moment than one movie at the cinema.

I should add that the people acting in Solvognen aren't interested in achieving recognition as artists. That's something the commercial bourgeois theatre world finds confusing. We believe in doing things on a collective basis, because what we want to convey is the play itself, not any actor in particular. But now Solvognen as a 'brand' is attracting the same kind of fame as a film star would, so we're thinking of giving up the name and starting again under a new one. We want to break down the boundaries around theatre.

Christiania itself is a kind of theatre and we are lucky to be part of it. We make use of the whole environment; we make our sets and print our posters in the workshops. The Grey Hall must be the most beautiful theatre in Denmark. Our play Elverhøj was seen by 25,000 people— they didn't all pay to get in because we believe people should only pay what they can afford.

A scene from the Moon Play, written by Jon Bang Carlsen and performed by Solvognen in 1976 in the Grey Hall. The moon was actually made for the 1974 Father Christmas action (see opposite). Its outline was fashioned from old water pipes welded together to support the canvas. Some communities recycle bottles—Solvognen recycled junk, turning waste into props, which were upcycled to appear in a new guise in later productions.

## THE FATHER CHRISTMAS ARMY

*This is a wonderful story Per Løvetand told me. I wish I'd been in Christiania when it happened, but in Per's account we can see how Christiania bridled at the modern world.*

It's Christmas time. Four hundred people in Christiania, inspired by Solvognen, make Father Christmas outfits. They pack them into shopping bags and walk to one of the big stores in Copenhagen. They split up and make their way to the toilets on each of the seven floors. It's been well rehearsed; the Christmas shoppers don't pay them any attention.

They quickly put on the Father Christmas outfits and head back to the crowded shopping aisles. The Father Christmas Army (as it became known) start to give away the items on sale: 'Here you are, take this—Happy Christmas.' The shop assistants join in, thinking it's a promotion arranged by the management, or perhaps just liking the idea of handing stuff out for free. People are leaving with armfuls of presents.

The managers call the police, who storm into the building and begin arresting the Father Christmases, including the ones paid to give out little toys to children queuing up at the grottos on each floor. 'NO! Don't arrest me,' they shout, 'I'm the real Father Christmas!' 'No, no, we're the real Father Christmases,' say the Father Christmas Army.' You can't tell them apart—how could you? Every Father Christmas is arrested and taken to the police station. There's not enough room for them all inside so they're lined up around the building. The police have inadvertently encircled themselves by the Father Christmas Army.

The next four pictures were all taken during Christiania's seventh birthday party. A wonderful celebration of theatre, music and dance.

# LET CHRISTIANIA LIVE

Demonstrating to keep Christiania open was almost a full-time job in the early years.

Take a thousand independent-minded people, mostly in their twenties or thirties, mostly single, who have at least a passing acquaintance with each other, bring them together as the sun goes down, in beautiful bars serving what is probably the best lager in the world, add brilliant home-grown bands and the pictures that follow may give you an idea of what you get: laughter, longing, loving, adventures, misadventures…

They were difficult pictures to take. Even the fastest film was not sensitive enough and flashlight was not acceptable; it was harsh and uncomfortable (especially for anyone who had sampled the wares on Pusher Street). Besides, flashlight didn't produce pictures that conveyed the atmosphere you experienced at night in the Freetown.

The solution was inspired by the extraordinary American photographer Arthur Fellig, more widely known by his pseudonym Weegee. He described taking black and white photographs with 'invisible flash'. I copied his technique, covering the flash tube with an infrared filter, which absorbs all the visible light while transmitting the infrared light we can't see. Kodak High Speed Infrared film, made for scientific applications, was sensitive to this 'invisible' infrared light. It produces a lovely effect; infrared light is reflected from the wet layer of the skin and this gives its subjects a romantic glow perfectly in keeping with my memories of those long-ago nights. That film is lost to us now; Kodak discontinued it in 2007.

But then, missing the colour of Christiania's night life, I decided to make a series of hand-coloured collages.

The inspiration for these pictures were Hindi film posters. I love those images—crazy, over-the-top representations of fantastic Bollywood movies. But there was another reason for this approach: collage was a form practised to great effect in Christiania. I thought it would be interesting to use this technique in the book.

These pictures came together quickly. I printed up photographs of people that would fit together, pasted the figures onto cardboard sheets and took them over to Joan Smith, a professional retoucher in the days before Photoshop. As a young woman, she had hand-coloured wedding photographs, which at that time were taken on black and white film. Conventional colour prints faded in those days, so those precious memories were given colour and a long life. I'd sit with her in her studio and choose the colours and watch as the pictures came alive. For this edition, I went back to the original artwork and had them scanned, so now these too are preserved from the ravages of time.

One thing I don't think anyone noticed: I had planned them in a sequence, dictated by the phases of the moon. Each image was crazier as it progressed from crescent to full moon. The sequence culminates, as it must, in two pictures from the Moonfisher bar. If you want the soundtrack, dig out Steely Dan's album, *Can't Buy a Thrill*, or Bob Dylan's *Street Legal*, and revisit the scene: fireworks blazing; dogs a-barking; lovers kissing; the Prince of Denmark demanding the return of his elephants—strange days and stranger nights; heavenly and disastrous.

Or as Rick Danko once said, 'Time has a way of making everything look bigger than it really is. Thank God for time.'[12]

12  Rick Danko is best known as a founding member of The Band. As everyone reading this book must know, they were one of the most influential and popular rock groups of all time and set a new standard for contemporary music.

The quote is lifted from another anniversary—a newly remastered (and not to be missed) DVD edition of *The 30th Anniversary Concert Celebration*. I've taken it straight out of Bill Flanagan's wonderful essay in the booklet that comes with the DVD.

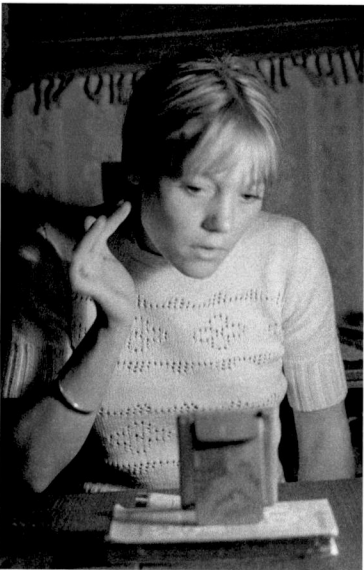

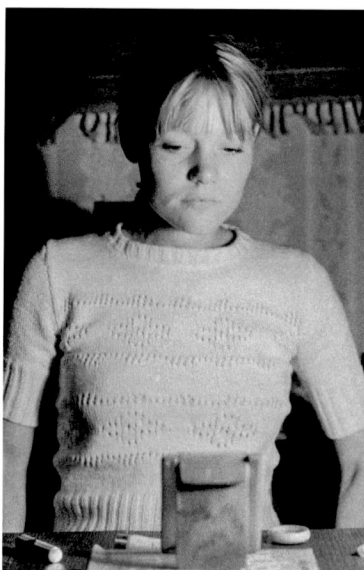

My neighbour Mette, getting ready for a night out in Christiania.

Light streaming into the Grey Hall illuminates a moment that captures the atmosphere of the times. It was actually taken on an earlier anniversary—Christiania's fifth birthday party—and was used as a poster when the first edition of *Christiania* was published.

Bazaar[13] playing in the Grey Hall, one of many wonderful evenings in this beautiful building. It dates from 1891 and was designed for officers to exercise and train their horses. When Christiania took over the barracks, it was transformed into the focal point for art, music and theatre. Bob Dylan famously played there, as did Rage Against the Machine, Metallica and Manic Street Preachers, but for sheer pleasure, it was hard to beat Bazaar.

The Grey Hall is also the venue for the Christmas market, organised with great skill by Putte (see page 86), and the venue for the Christmas Eve feast. At the time this book was written, posters advertising the Christmas party were displayed all over Copenhagen inviting everyone along—even God. The feast was paid for by the hash dealers. If God did turn up, He—or She—kept a low profile to enjoy a superb meal, followed by music and dance. It would surely have been a welcome change to the usual offerings.

If you really want to get an idea of the atmosphere, call up Pieter Bruegel's pictures of festivals painted five centuries earlier. Why? Because they are more human and more generous than anyone else's paintings of community life, and somehow, Christiania brought them alive again to show that the human spirit can surface in the modern world to celebrate life with all its troubles and joys. There is a lesson here at a time when democracy is threatened by populism and multinationals; when climate change, pollution, overpopulation, poverty and the destruction of natural systems demand a radically new, worldwide approach. If we don't celebrate being alive, we will never find the way to tackle the huge problems that shadow civilisation.

13  Bazaar wasn't a Christiania band, but they had close connections to the Freetown, frequently performing in the music venues and collaborating with Solvognen. They stopped performing in 2012.

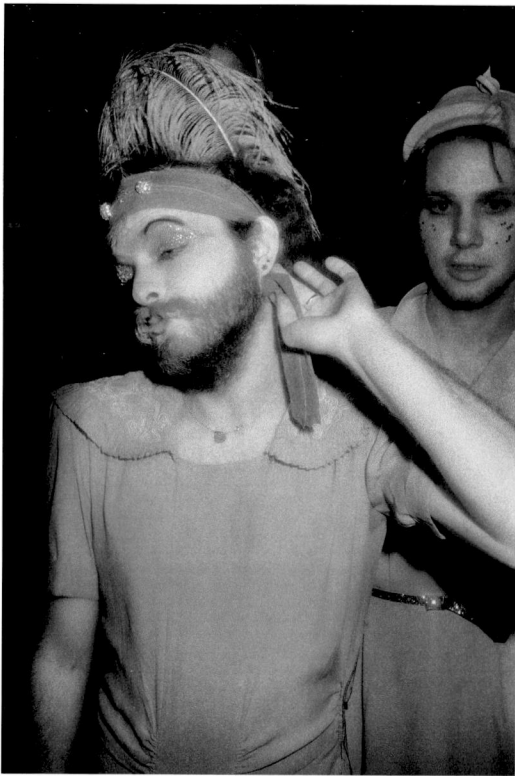

The Gay Liberation Front's party in the Grey Hall. The Gay Liberation Front is headquartered in Christiania.

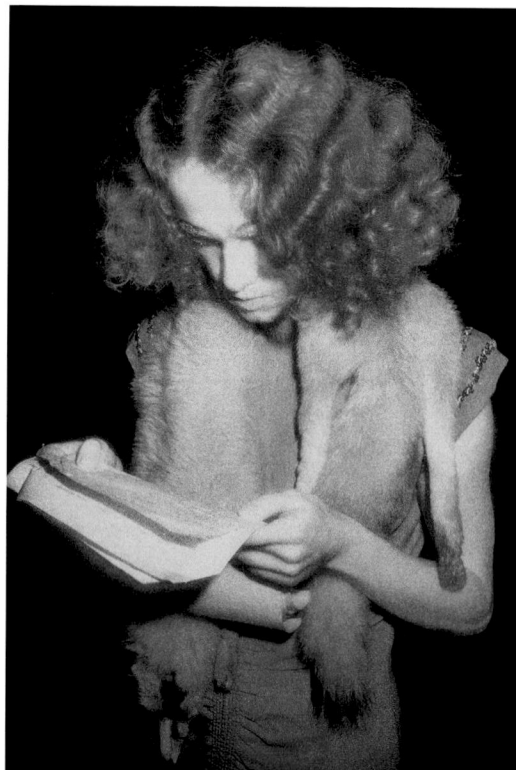

Loppen, Christiania's extraordinary night club. The ever-friendly Benny Larsen and his superhuman crew kept it rolling. It is so easy to take everything for granted, so this is a chance to give thanks for all their hard work.

I hesitated before I took this picture; was I stepping over that invisible, but very real line to cause offence? These are the kinds of situation that haunt photographers; you see a picture just waiting to be framed, but is it out of bounds? We want pictures that reflect intimacy, drama—all the human emotions—but there are limits to intrusion. Sometimes those limits are clear, and you walk away (as I did on several occasions in Christiania). Sometimes you take the picture and get it wrong. Sometimes you walk away and wish you hadn't.

To make it more difficult, the limits change with each generation. Photographers are more restricted now than in the 1970s, the period that this book describes. And behaviour changes; the casual, public nakedness in many of the photos I took in Christiania is not to be seen now.

Obviously, I had to decide pretty quickly if I was to catch this moment—it wasn't a pose that was going to last too long. I decided to walk around the building, and if they were still in each other's arms when I got back, I'd press the button. Well, here it is, a risky picture, justified, perhaps, because I'm the only person who knows who the couple are. Their secret is safe with me!

# CHRISTIANIA IN THE WORLD

Reissued albums aren't complete without a few bonus tracks. So, with a tip of the hat to the music world, I include a few pictures of Christianites outside the confines of the Freetown. All of them, except the first one, were taken after the original edition was published.

# REHEARSAL FOR THE YEAR 2000

I took these pictures for the cover of Nicholas Albery's autobiography with the snappy title: *Rehearsal for the Year 2000. The Rebirth of Albion Free State—Memoirs of a Male Midwife 1966—1976*[14]

Nicholas was a social inventor and author, who participated in the labour pains of the birth of the New Age. He conceded in 1976 that it was still not quite born. Detractors said it was a phantom pregnancy but that didn't stop Nicholas staging the future he believed in. He planned these photos as an 'undress rehearsal' for Timothy Leary's vision of pastureland in Piccadilly, a transformation Leary predicted for the year 2000. That deadline came and went, a reminder of just how easy it is to get dates wrong when you're on LSD.

A goat and a cockerel were borrowed from an urban farm in north London, and a group of friends were co-opted to meet at dawn, and stroll, naked, across the future green pastures of Piccadilly Circus.

Nicholas is seen here with his partner, Josefine, and their baby Merlyn (and the borrowed goat) on the left. Ebba, from Den Kosmiske Blomst, can just be seen behind Nick Saunders, who in 1976 was a frequent visitor to Christiania.

But there is an unsettling hint of the future in these pictures. The coronavirus pandemic emptied London's streets for much of 2020. Piccadilly wasn't deserted long enough for grass to grow through the tarmac, but it was a vivid reminder that our headlong collision with nature has the potential to do terrible damage to civilisation. For many people in the West, Covid-19 was the first personal encounter with the biodiversity crisis—as we reach into nature's habitats, we are exposed to new viruses against which we have no natural immunity.

In the damaged environment, we glimpse the limits of the modern world. We see ourselves dependent on nature's extraordinary diversity, which defies the elementary mechanism we've tried to impose. Our arrogant simplicity has been challenged by nature's awesome—but delicate—complexity. We've been short-sighted—the ecological equivalent of friendly fire.

Perhaps the pandemic will give us a new sense of urgency to tackle our environmental problems. It is an unprecedented opportunity to rethink what we really want for ourselves and for the world at large.

But don't count on it; politicians, like most of humanity, are good at ignoring the long-term threats to our security.

---

14  Nicholas Albery was wonderful company and is very sadly missed; he died in 2001 in a car accident. *Rehearsal for the Year 2000* was written under one of his many pseudonyms, Alan Bean. He reviewed it for the back-cover blurb under another name and did so very critically. It was printed on a borrowed Xerox machine in Neal's Yard. A reprint is long overdue.

The Christiania can-can girls waiting nervously to perform on stage at a long-forgotten venue in town.

I took these pictures after I escaped from a police cell in Russia. I'd gone to Leningrad for the *Observer* magazine. I was arrested, accused of spying and locked up. A KGB officer was sent for and arrived with a very attractive young woman to translate. At one point I asked her to say to my interrogator, 'Look at me—do you really think I look like a spy?' He thought for a moment and replied, 'We know you know everything.' As someone with a learning difficulty (I'm dyslexic), this was music to my ears. I felt a surge of confidence course through me and gave more and more detailed answers.

It was getting late, and he fell sleep. The beautiful interpreter told me the keys were on a clip on his belt. 'Listen, 007, if you unlock the door, I'll take you to your hotel. (Another surge of confidence…) Tomorrow I'll put you on a train to Finland.' This is not the place for the full reveal, but it did give me a fascinating insight into Russia in 1982.

I got safely to Finland and decided to return home via Copenhagen. When I arrived in Denmark, the first Copenhagen Carnival was just getting under way. Christianites who had so long filled the role of court jester to the nation were surrounded by a city in fancy dress, dancing day and night in an exhibition of unalloyed merriment that rivalled the wildest nights in the Freetown.

Christiania, for once outnumbered at the party, rose magnificently to the challenge. It was a wonderful occasion, and these pictures are included here to demonstrate that we all value the opportunity to celebrate community life, not just as spectators, but as whole-hearted participants. I took out my camera and the film I should have used in Russia and had the time of my life capturing the fun and mishaps. It was a far cry from the police cell in Leningrad.[15]

PS. Apologies if I've mixed up Christianites and Copenhageners! Not only am I looking back across nearly forty years with a very human memory, but everyone was in disguise.

---

15 Borgen Forlag published a selection of my pictures taken at Copenhagen Carnival in 1982.

This small bonus chapter ends in another wonderful playground, Tivoli, with Hjelta, Nina and their children on a day out. They were among the first people to welcome me into their home in Christiania and have remained firm friends ever since.

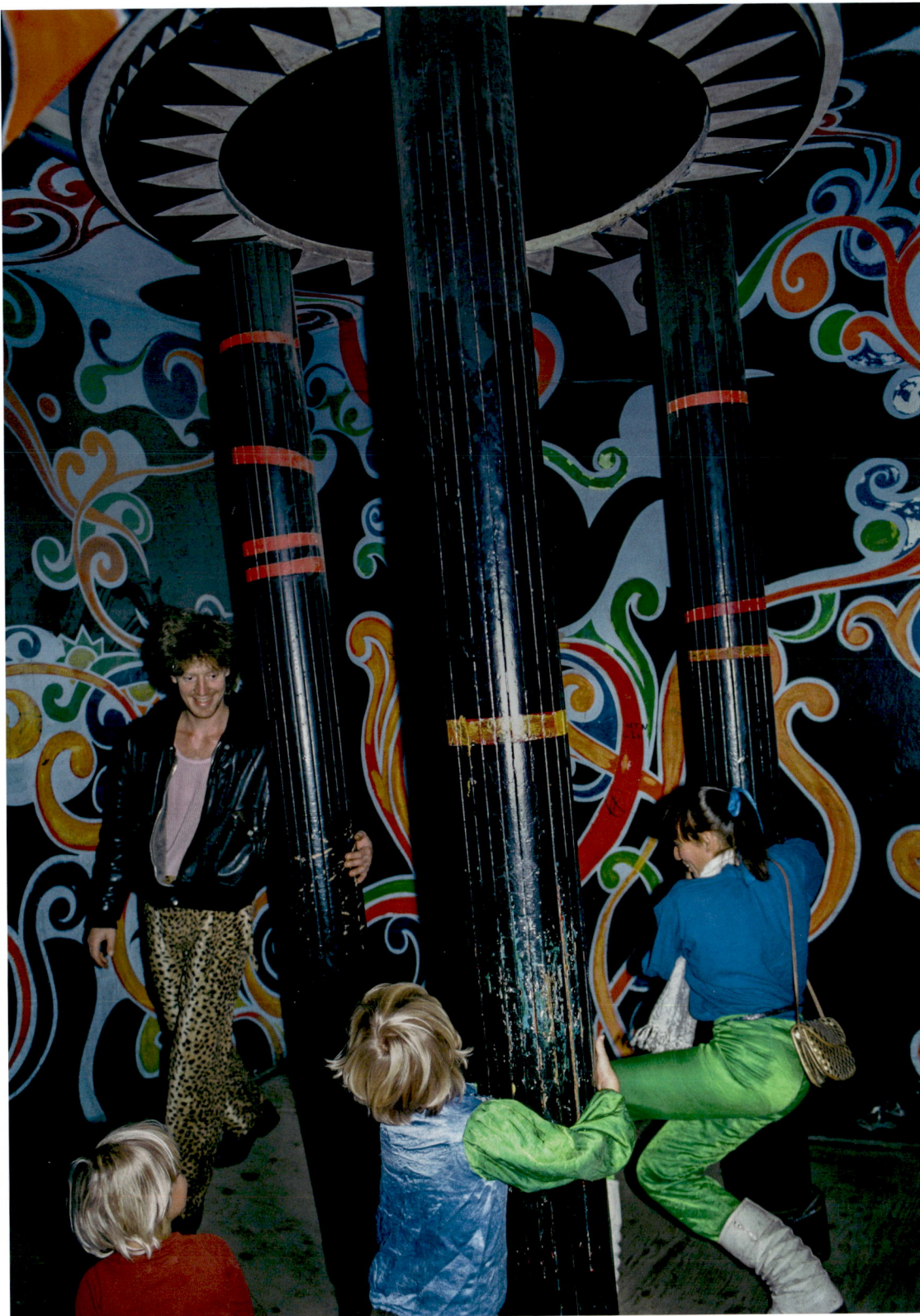

The first I heard of Christiania was in 1975 in Nicholas Saunders' home in Edith Grove, west London.

Nick was a leading figure in the alternative movement. He had self-published the best-selling book *Alternative London*, a guidebook for people living on the fringes of conventional society with 'alternative' values and ambitions. At this time thousands of people were squatting empty houses in London, even whole streets in the 1970s, and Nick's book provided the practical advice needed to take over empty houses and make them liveable. It was packed with tips and advice on how to live well with little money.

He had turned his front room into a papier-mâché cave. There was space for a dozen people to sit on cushions around a jigsaw-puzzle-shaped table facing a plate-glass window which looked on to a pond. His ducks could dive below the bottom edge of the glass and climb on to the table and join us whenever they wanted human company—or to escape foxes. They were always welcome.

That evening, Ebba,[16] a young woman living in Christiania, held us spellbound with her account of the Freetown. It sounded like alternative heaven. Nick was keen to make a booklet focusing on the practical aspects of life there. I was to take the photos. We set off to Harwich to board the ferry to Esbjerg a week later.

We arrived at Christiania's main gate on a cold, dark evening and walked across the border dividing the Freetown from Copenhagen. It was like stepping back a thousand years. It looked awful; it was dirty, dogs were barking, people were shouting, but we followed the map Ebba had made for us to the bridge over the lake and met her in her beautiful room. This was a place of contrasts.

We went to Loppen, one of Christiania's concert venues, later that evening. A brilliant band played through the night. Everyone knew each other so it was like a huge friendly but edgy party. I quickly realised I had a major problem to overcome; people didn't like being photographed. I had to tread very, very carefully, but I quite liked the challenge of winning people over to our project.

We returned in February and again in March 1976. Each time I brought pictures I'd taken earlier and gave them out to the people I'd photographed.[17] Slowly, as I got to know a wider circle of people, I assumed the role of Christiania's unofficial photographer. They understood that this was to be a permanent record of the way this unique community developed.

Funding was to be a major preoccupying problem. Between 1975 and 1979, I made fifteen separate visits to Christiania, living there for eighteen months in total. My costs ran to £8000. If I'd been Danish, I might have got grants from Danish foundations; if Christiania had been in Britain, I might have got grants from British foundations.

Nick, however, found an ingenious way of covering our travel costs. He noticed that butter was twice as expensive in Denmark as in Britain, where the government had maintained a butter subsidy. On the way to the ferry, we'd stock up with Lurpak butter, pack it into boxes arranged like seats around Nick's truck and smuggle it back into Denmark. Indkøbscentralen (the general store) bought it all. In this way, we provided the Freetown with cut-price butter and covered the cost of our travel.

It worked brilliantly in winter but the summer trips were nerve-wracking; would our expensive cargo melt before we reached Christiania? Then suddenly the price of butter in the UK caught up with Denmark. Nick came to the rescue once again. He noticed that Brazil nuts had a luxury tax applied in Denmark, so we switched from Lurpak to huge sacks of Brazils. These were again arranged around the truck and covered with rugs and we were back in business. Not liking an empty truck on the way home, we offered trips from Christiania to Covent Garden for £10, hiding our passengers under the rugs before we drove on to the ferry. We'd even discovered how to use empty cabins, so we offered a luxury crossing for the price of a few beers.

You'd think people who were stowaways would keep a low profile. Not a bit of it. Our companions emerged from the truck, slightly flushed, and made their way up to the deck, throwing fire, and giving free impromptu theatre shows for the rest of the passengers.

Those journeys deserve a book of their own, but you can't photograph everything that happens in your life.

The switch to Brazil nuts had far-reaching consequences. It gave

---

16 Co-author of *With Love, Siri and Ebba*, an astonishing account by Siri Fraser and Ebba Pedersen of hitch-hiking through Africa to Sudan and Ethiopia where they lived 'with the most fantastic free wild nomadic tribes'. It was published by Nicholas Saunders, compiled from letters and drawings he and other friends received from them during their adventure. It was launched at Heathrow Airport, much to their surprise, as they arrived back in London.

17 Some of these work prints survive and have been uploaded to a Facebook page. Ironically, I was banned from Facebook—some of the Christiania pictures I uploaded were of naked people and were censored. It's another reminder of how times have changed.

Nick the idea for Neal's Yard, now a famous landmark in London. I was driving the truck, weighed down with nuts, while Nick sat next to me with a calculator, working out the profit margin on health foods when wholesale quantities were repacked for shops. He was appalled at the mark-up they charged. He had the idea to offer whole foods in bulk, in simple packaging with the smallest mark-up possible. We were driving past Maryland Station in Stratford, east London when the idea came together.

At this point Nick's interest in the Christiania booklet faded, though he remained very supportive of the project. His energy went into setting up the Whole Food Warehouse. It was soon joined by a bakery, a coffee shop and a cheese shop in what had been a derelict courtyard in Covent Garden. Nick would set up each new enterprise, and when he had the right people in place, he'd make the business over to them. Neal's Yard stands as a tribute to this remarkable man. He died in a car crash in South Africa in 1998 and is still greatly missed.

I now had the opportunity to focus on making a more ambitious, picture-led book with text dictated by Christiania's inhabitants. I set out to document all aspects of life in the Freetown; to try to convey the spirit of the place and show what it was like to live there.

At this time my life was divided between Christiania, London and assignments for magazines and UN agencies in Asia, Africa and South America. I lived by turn in remote rural villages and shanty towns in the Majority World, with indigenous people in jungles and deserts, then back to my darkroom in London and on to more adventures in Christiania. I was witnessing human nature in all our contradictory glory.

I was also very fortunate in meeting Per Kofod from Informations Forlag, a small publishing company that made a contribution to publishing out of all proportion to its size. Their generous advance allowed me to spend additional time in Christiania taping conversations about life there. When the interviews were finished, I sent all the cassettes off to a friend in London who had agreed to transcribe them. She lost the lot and stupidly I'd not made copies. After a very anxious period, they turned up in a London squat, just days before the police evicted everyone and everything.

Per left the publishing house before the book went to the printers. Sadly, the printing was appalling; the black and white pictures looked like cheap newsprint. The company agreed they had let us down but would not withdraw the copies and reprint the book. After all the work and effort, I could hardly bring myself to look at it. Later, a better printed German edition helped make up for the disappointment. There was also to be an English edition but just before it went to press the small publisher went out of business.

Christiania's 50th anniversary prompted me to look at the pictures and interviews again. I wrote to Rane Willerslev, Director at the National Museum of Denmark, to see if he might be interested in an exhibition. I offered the museum the original films, work prints and recordings, which I thought they might be interested in as a record of the early years of the Freetown. After several months, I called to make sure they had received the letter and prints I'd sent. I was told they'd arrived but hadn't been passed on to Rane and that neither he nor anyone else would look at them or even consider the proposal.

My friend Barry Pringle, a photographer and long-time resident of Copenhagen, kindly collected the prints and took them to a wonderful gallery in the centre of town. They offered to host the exhibition and invited me to a meeting to see the space. We agreed the exhibition layout and the launch dates, and I got to work scanning the pictures. Unfortunately, they had forgotten to mention that they would charge a very considerable sum to hire the gallery. By the time they realised their mistake, I'd paid for the scans, already a substantial investment. Their additional charge was way beyond my budget. With great disappointment, I had to pull out.

The *Christiania* book, like its subject, has a chequered history! Now I have the scans, the text and the time to make a new edition of the book, which will ensure better printing quality than in the original edition. More importantly, Mike Kenny was willing to revive the original design and Kristina Blagojevitch to carefully edit out the inevitable rough edges from a spoken text delivered in a foreign language.

# ACKNOWLEDGEMENTS

First of all, huge thanks to Christiania's original pioneers for letting me photograph the Freetown.

I made a point of staying in different areas on each visit. That way I kept meeting new communities within Christiania. It served to remind me that generalisations about Christianites are only true in a limited sense. It was then, and surely is now, a very diverse community and I am very grateful to the many friends who let me stay with them. There are too many to name, but your hospitality and kindness all those years ago made this book possible.

I owe a sidelong debt of gratitude to the coronavirus pandemic and the inept handling of the crisis in the UK by prime minister Boris Johnson. He and his dithering ministers meant we were locked down for longer than would have been the case if they'd acted decisively early in the outbreak. This gave me more time to work on this new edition.

Huge thanks to Magnum photographer Chris Steele-Perkins. Chris is a friend of long standing and was always the first to see the photographs when I returned from trips to the Freetown. He helped separate the wheat from the chaff and he urged me to revisit the project for this 50th anniversary edition.

Special thanks to Hjalte Tin for advice and encouragement with both editions of Christiania and to Lise Autogena, Judith Morgan, Ralf Køpke, Lloyd Timberlake, Emmerik Warburg, Bojan Brecelj, Julio Etchart, Inger Sølling, Ole Lykke, Britta Lillesøe and Nils Vest for help in completing this book.

Barry Pringle deserves a special mention; a friend from our student days at Guildford School of Art, he moved to Copenhagen many years ago and helped with contacts in Denmark. Many thanks, Barry.

Stu Culley set me up with an Imacon scanner (another brilliant Danish invention), which brought the original negatives back to life.

Chloe Rosser helped me get to grips with the retouching tools on Lightroom® and took over the controls when the adjustments were beyond my limited abilities. Chloe also created the website, so she has been up to her eyes in the 1970s counterculture and has survived unscathed.

When we were faced with a blizzard of dust and scratches that high-end scanners pick up on the pictures, I turned to Alex Roy and his team at Unigate Systems (India). They sent the images back without a blemish. Thank you one and all.

Brexit prevented me from using the UK printers I have worked with in the past. LUart, based in Slovenia, stepped into the breach. Igor Stanonik must be one of Europe's leading print experts and could not have been more helpful.

Kristina Blagojevitch lightly re-edited the interviews and commentaries, bringing them alive for a new audience.

Ida Dam Juutilainen very kindly went through a folder of faded press cuttings that were published when the original edition of Christiania first appeared. She found the quotes included on the flap.

Mike Kenny has retained the beautiful design Dennis Bailey produced for Informations Forlag in the original edition of Christiania but has brought his own judgement to many of the pages. It was, as always, a pleasure to work with him on this project, even though we could not meet up or have lunch at the Chelsea Arts Club.

Dennis Bailey was a graduate from the Royal College of Art and was one of the foremost graphic designers in the UK. We met when we were both teaching at Chelsea College of Art, and I was privileged to collaborate with him on several projects. After completing the first edition of Christiania, Dennis and fellow graphic designer Mike Kenny worked together on a wide variety of projects until Dennis died in 2016.

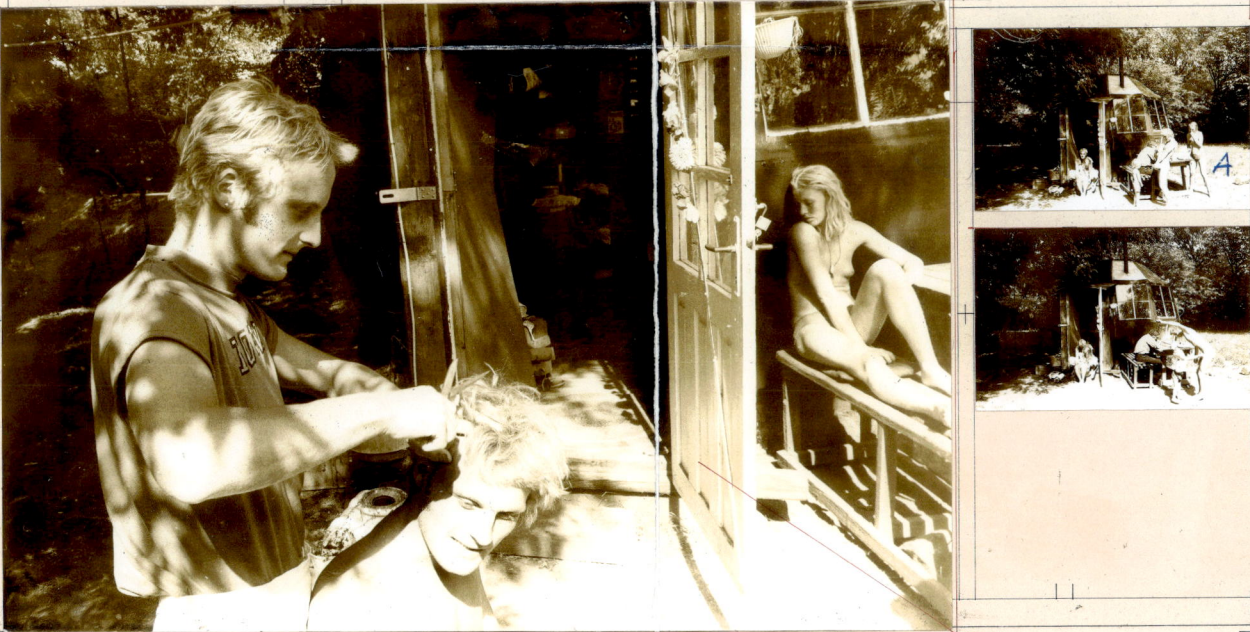

CHRISTIANIA PICTURE BOOK 228 x 238mm
photos & text: Mark Edwards
design: Dennis Bailey

One of the original page layouts produced by Dennis Bailey. It reflects his meticulous approach to design.

Visit www.christiania.co.uk to view the pictures and text and to order copies of the book…

...posters and postcards.

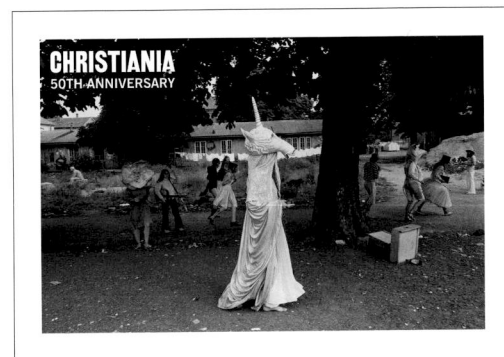